UNITED NATIONS CONFERENCE ON TRADE AND DEVELOPMENT

POLICY ISSUES IN INTERNATIONAL TRADE AND COMMODITIES

STUDY SERIES No. 5

TARIFFS, TAXES AND ELECTRONIC COMMERCE:

REVENUE IMPLICATIONS FOR DEVELOPING COUNTRIES

by

Susanne Teltscher

UNCTAD
Palais des Nations
1211 Geneva 10, Switzerland
susan.teltscher@unctad.org

UNITED NATIONS

New York and Geneva, 2000

NOTE

The views expressed in this study are those of the author and do not necessarily reflect the views of the United Nations.

The designations employed and the presentation of the material do not imply the expression of any opinion whatsoever on the part of the United Nations Secretariat concerning the legal status of any country, territory, city or area, or of its authorities, or concerning the delimitation of its frontiers or boundaries.

Material in this publication may be freely quoted or reprinted, but acknowledgement is requested, together with a reference to the document number. A copy of the publication containing the quotation or reprint should be sent to the UNCTAD secretariat:

Chief
Trade Analysis Branch
Division on International Trade in Goods and Services, and Commodities
United Nations Conference on Trade and Development
Palais des Nations
CH – 1211 Geneva

UN2 TD) UNCTAD/ITCD/TAB/5

UNCTAD/ITCD/TAB/5

UNITED NATIONS PUBLICATION
Sales No. E.00.II.D.36
ISBN 92-1-112505-7
ISSN 1607-8291

ABSTRACT

Cross-border electronic commerce is currently operating in a tax- and tariff-free environment. This, combined with predictions of steep increases of e-commerce during the next five years, has prompted Governments and tax authorities to discuss modifications to existing legislation that take account of these developments. One of their concerns is the potential loss in tax and tariff revenues resulting from e-commerce, which account for significant shares of government budgets in most countries. This is of particular concern to developing countries, where import duties comprise higher shares of government revenue and a shift to other revenue sources is economically less feasible. The paper presents data on potential revenue losses from import duties on a number of products that have been traded physically in the past but are increasingly being imported digitally. Findings show that developing countries will be the main losers as far as import duties from e-commerce products are concerned, while both developing and developed countries would suffer major revenue cuts from lost consumption taxes.

ACKNOWLEDGEMENTS

I am very grateful to Hiroaki Kuwahara for his contribution to the tariff and trade data analysis, and to Florence Cuenod Guenin for her assistance in collecting the import duty data. Bijit Bora, Erich Supper and Christopher Stevens provided useful comments on earlier versions of the paper.

CONTENTS

INTRODUCTION

The most debated topic in electronic commerce at the present time, both among policy makers and the business community, is whether and how to collect tariffs and taxes on cross-border electronic commerce (e-commerce). So far, no national or international legislation has been put in place. At the same time, a steep increase in e-commerce during the next decade is predicted: the Organisation for Economic Co-operation and Development (OECD) estimates that it may reach a value of US$ 330 billion by 2001–2002 and US$ 1 trillion by 2003–2005 (OECD, 1999b). According to Forrester Research estimates, business-to-business e-commerce accounted for US$ 150 billion in 1999. This is expected to reach over US$ 3 trillion by 2004 (The Economist, 2000b). Hence, there is legitimate concern by Governments, especially in the developing countries, over the potential erosion of their tax base resulting from e-commerce if domestic and international rules are not modified to take account of these developments.

Data on government finance statistics support this concern (Table 1 and Figure 1). They show that taxes are the principal source of government revenue, accounting on average for about 80 per cent of total revenue (all countries). Domestic taxation of goods and services makes up the largest share in tax revenues (36.5 per cent).[1] Revenues from import duties account on average for 13.2 per cent of total revenue and 17.5 per cent of tax revenue. Major differences exist between developing and developed countries: for the former, import duties as a share of total government revenue are 15.8 per cent (compared with 2.6 per cent for developed countries) and as a share of tax revenue 21.2 per cent (compared with 3 per cent for developed countries).[2] The combined tax revenues from

goods and services and those from imports account for 54 per cent of tax revenues (all countries), or 58.3 per cent of developing countries' and 37 per cent of developed countries' tax revenue. Hence, they make up a major source of government revenue in most countries.[3]

How will these revenues be affected by e-commerce? Will the increase in digital trade substantially reduce revenues from import duties and taxation of domestic goods and services? Should e-commerce therefore be subject to border tariffs and taxes?

The question of whether to levy tariffs on cross-border e-commerce has been taken up by the World Trade Organization (WTO). In 1998, WTO member States agreed to a two-year customs duties moratorium on "electronic transmissions". A decision on whether to extend the moratorium should have been taken at the Third WTO Ministerial Meeting[4] but has been postponed.

The broader subject of Internet taxation has been taken up by other forums. A number of proposals are currently being prepared by the OECD, the European Union and the United States for harmonizing taxation rules on international e-commerce and thus prevent

---

member countries do not report revenues from import duties (some report very low values). This is because EU import duties are directly passed on to the EU common budget as a traditional own resources payment, and only 10 per cent is retained by the importing country (this share will be increased to 25 per cent as of 2001). Therefore, the calculations of EU member States' import revenues are based on their individual contributions to the EU budget (European Commission, 1998).

[3] Other important sources not considered here are income taxes and social security contributions.

[4] The Third WTO Ministerial Meeting was held in Seattle from 30 November to 1 December 1999.

---

[1] Mainly sales and value added taxes.

[2] In the case of the European Union, individual

potential fiscal losses that could result from a rapidly growing number of international on-line suppliers, whose cross-border transactions will be subject to import and domestic taxes.

Developing countries are largely left out of these debates. Within the WTO, they have raised concerns about possible tariff revenue implications resulting from a ban on customs duties on electronic transmissions. However, they lack resources to provide evidence which could support their concerns. Many of them are still struggling to keep up with the rapid developments in the area of e-commerce, recognizing that it has the potential for substantial beneficial effects on their economies.[5] The taxation debate is very much dominated by the OECD countries, which have little concern for developing countries' interests, given the latter's small share in e-commerce. However, developing countries could be much more affected by fiscal losses resulting from e-commerce in view of their greater dependence on tariffs and taxes as revenue sources for their national budgets.

This paper attempts to bring the developing countries' concerns into the debate on potential revenue implications of e-commerce by looking at both tariff and tax revenues. Section II provides a short overview of the discussion on border tariffs for e-commerce taking place in the WTO. Key to this debate are conceptual and regulatory aspects of imposing customs duties on electronic transmissions. Section III looks at Internet taxation issues such as consumption and income taxation. Section four moves to the empirical part of the paper. It first analyses, using trade and tariff revenue data, the potential economic impact if in fact digitizable products replace physically delivered goods. Particular attention is paid to the impact on developing countries. This is followed by an analysis of

additional duties levied on imports (besides border tariffs), including domestic consumption taxes (section V). On this basis, possible revenue losses resulting from e-commerce, particularly in the developing countries, are shown.

---

[5] For a discussion on e-commerce and development, see ITU (1999).

I. IMPORT TARIFFS AND CLASSIFICATION OF E-COMMERCE

The Geneva Ministerial Declaration of May 1998 includes for the first time in GATT/WTO history a mandate for work in the area of e-commerce. It specifies two elements: first, a standstill agreement on the imposition of customs duties on electronic transmissions; and second, a General Council mandate to establish a work programme on global electronic commerce. Four WTO bodies (the Council for Trade in Services, the Council for Trade in Goods, the Council for Trade-Related Aspects of Intellectual Property Rights and the Committee for Trade and Development) were thus instructed to examine and report on different aspects of e-commerce.[6] Although member States decided that all aspects concerning the imposition of customs duties on e-commerce would be examined in the General Council, the four WTO bodies had to address customs duties when discussing the classification of e-commerce, or more specifically, of electronic transmissions. "Classification" broadly refers to the question of whether electronic transmissions, or products shipped electronically (instead of physically), should be characterized as goods, services, intellectual property or something else. It is thus an issue that cuts across the debates in all four bodies. So far, no agreement has been reached. In fact, the difficulty of finding an agreement on the classification question has held up progress in the work on e-commerce, especially in the Council for Trade in Goods.

The link between the classification issue and the ban on customs duties is simple: depending on how electronic transmissions are defined, different multilateral agreements apply. For example, if they were classified as goods, they would be subject to General Agreement on Tariffs and Trade (GATT) rules, which would make electronically shipped products dutiable. If they were classified as services, on the other hand, they would be subject to General Agreement on Trade in Services (GATS) rules, and the application of customs duties would be questionable. This, in turn, would have different implications for government revenues obtained from tariffs imposed on these goods. Several WTO member States have therefore suggested that a final decision on the extension of the customs ban be delayed until the classification issue has been solved. The following will take a closer look at the conceptual and regulatory issues related to the classification of e-commerce (and hence the imposition of border tariffs), and how existing multilateral rules address them.

A. Conceptual issues

In the Geneva Ministerial Declaration, Ministers "also declare that Members will continue their current practice of not imposing customs duties on electronic transmissions". In order to fully understand the meaning and implications of this decision, the terms "customs duties" and "electronic transmissions" deserve further consideration.

The decision on the ban on customs duties is based on a proposal submitted by the United States in February 1998 to the General Council, noting that "currently, no Member of the WTO

---

[6] Since 1998, each body has held a number of meetings where Members discussed and made proposals on the issues relevant to the work programme. By the end of July 1999, each body had submitted a progress report to the General Council. These reports have been reviewed by the General Council and were to be used for submitting recommendations to the Seattle Ministerial Conference for decision. The Seattle Conference, however, did not address the subject of e-commerce and a decision has been postponed until negotiations restart in Geneva. At the General Council meeting of 17 July 2000 Members decided that the four WTO bodies should continue their work on e-commerce, including the identification of cross-sectoral issues. They will report back to the General Council in December 2000. The question of the extension of the customs ban has been put aside.

considers electronic transmissions as importations for customs duties purposes and, thus, not one imposes customs duties on them" (WTO, 1998). Therefore, according to the United States, "WTO Members should agree to continue this current practice so that the absence of customs duties on electronic transmissions would remain". Thus, the proposal, first, suggests that electronic transmissions are not considered as importations by countries; and, second, implies indirectly that electronic transmissions could theoretically be considered as importations in the sense of GATT Article II. They would therefore be subject to tariffs. This contradiction is at the heart of the debate at WTO: on the one hand, it is not clear whether electronic transmissions should be regarded as an importation of goods and therefore fall under the GATT; on the other hand, the term "customs duties" suggests that an importation is actually taking place.

Customs duties in the traditional GATT/WTO sense imply the importation of a good, which could then be subject to border tariffs (GATT, 1986). The World Customs Organization (WCO) Harmonized System of Classification and Description of Goods (HS) codes are applied to these importations at the international level. Imports that cannot be classified under the HS coding system (e.g. services) are not subject to border tariffs. Customs duties on imports do not normally include domestic taxes on goods or services; rather, these remain a domain of national policy. On the other hand, most countries levy some additional duties and taxes on imported goods. These include excise taxes, value-added taxes, consumption taxes and other fees, some of which are being equivalent to taxes charged on domestically produced and sold goods (and services). Hence, it is necessary to define clearly the term "customs duties": does it merely refer to most-favoured-nation border tariffs (the GATT meaning) or does it also refer to additional customs duties and taxes imposed on imports? In the latter case, the discussion would clearly move into the area of domestic taxation. This is why

some people have confused the issue of whether electronic transmissions should be subject to domestic taxes with the proposed ban on customs duties.[7] Section IV will discuss and provide empirical evidence on additional customs duties levied on imports.

A second important element in any further discussion at the WTO is the definition of electronic transmissions, i.e. whether the "digits" transmitted over the Internet should be classified as goods, services, or something else. For certain electronic transactions, an agreement could be reached fairly easily. For example, goods that have been ordered, paid for or marketed electronically but shipped physically are clearly goods in the traditional sense and all relevant agreements (such as the GATT) would apply. Similarly, the supply of (traditional) services via electronic means would clearly fall under the GATS. They include financial services, accountancy, tourism, computer-related and back-office services, educational and, of course, telecommunications services.

The most controversial debate concerns the electronic transmission of data which have physical counterparts, e.g. books, music, film and video material, and software (WTO, 1999b, 1999d, 1999e). In the past, these products were shipped physically via carrier media such as CDs, diskettes and tapes. They were physically moved across borders, where they were subject to import duties. Today, and increasingly so in the future, they are being sent via data files through virtual networks, thereby crossing numerous (sometimes unknown) borders. The data are then downloaded onto a carrier medium, printed or stored on a computer. They could be sent to individuals for direct consumption or to retailers for distribution.

How should these data or their content be classified? Are they equivalent to a hard copy of

---

[7] See, for example, *Wall Street Journal*, Europe, 7 October 1999.

4

a book or catalogue, a CD or videotape and therefore to be classified as a "good"? Is the transmission of the data itself a service and should the "data" thus fall under the services category? Or should there be a third category of electronic transmissions, some mixture of goods and services? But, in that case, which would be the governing multilateral rules? The following raises a number of issues that should be taken into consideration when deciding on a possible classification of electronic transmissions:

- According to the traditional WTO definition, a good would be a trade where the end product can be converted into a "tangible" or physical product; a service would be an end product that is "intangible", i.e. it cannot be converted into a physical good. However, given that electronic products can be stored in electronic or intangible form, some WTO Members have suggested that there could be a new category of "intangible goods"; here the GATT would apply, as opposed to "intangible services", where the GATS would apply. The criteria for these "intangible goods" remain to be defined.

- Clarification is needed on whether downloaded data could fall under the definition of an import (WTO, 1999c). This is important since the GATT and customs duties apply only in the case of an importation. Is there something that actually moves across borders, in the sense of an importation according to Article II of the GATT? Are the data carried by a carrier medium (e.g. a CD) also an importation or only the carrier itself? Currently, these data are subject to import duties if they are imported via a carrier medium (which is still the case for the large majority of media and software products).

- Should a distinction be made between the mass distribution of electronically transmitted goods and personalized distribution? For example, if a commercial catalogue is sent electronically to a publisher

overseas where it will be printed and distributed, should it not be subject to customs duties like its physical counterpart? On the other hand, if an individual buyer requests and receives advertising material on a specific product from the manufacturer, should this not be defined as a service? In the former, the GATT would apply, in the latter the GATS would apply.

- Rather than being a good, could not the "content" of the digital transmission be intellectual property? For example, in the case of software, the value is not the actual product but rather the licensing fee paid to the manufacturer. This relates to the question of to what extent the HS system can be applied to electronic transmissions. So far, the HS identifies the relevant products together with the carrying media, and not separately. Should there be HS codes for "intangible goods"?[8]

- One useful suggestion has been to define electronic transmissions as goods if they (a) can be locally stored and (b) are transferable (Drake and Nicolaidis, 1999).[9] "Locally stored" here refers to the possibility of downloading the product onto a physical media, even if it does not have a tangible form (i.e. if it is downloaded onto a computer). "Transferable" refers to the possibility of preserving the value of the product independently of the initial consumer and transferring it to another consumer without the intervention of the producer.

---

[8] It should be noted that the HS coding system includes a heading for electrical energy (27.16), clearly an "intangible good". However, the use of this heading is optional, i.e. it is left to the discretion of the HS Contracting Parties. Because of the disagreement among WCO member States on the question of software, the WCO decided not to introduce three new HS codes to classify software in its 2002 revision of the HS system, as had been originally foreseen.

[9] This definition is similar to that of goods and services made by Hill (1977).

These two criteria would clearly distinguish electronic goods from services and may be better suited than traditional criteria, such as inclusion in the HS commodity system, tangible or intangible character of the good, etc.

Three points clearly emerge from the above discussion. First, the classification issue requires moving beyond traditional definitions in order to account for new technologies that have transformed the original concept of goods and services. Second, it would be oversimplistic to define all electronic transmissions as services, given the obvious likeness between, for example, an article or a movie downloaded from the Internet and a journal or videotape bought at a store. Finally, no matter how these products will eventually be defined, a number of them, which currently form part of customs schedules and are thus subject to import tariffs, will be likely to fall under different import regulations in the future. The question of potential revenue losses thus remains valid in all cases.

B.   Regulatory issues

Within the WTO context, there are also important political and regulatory implications associated with the electronic delivery of goods and services. Depending on the classification, the trade is subject to different multilateral rules: goods are subject to the GATT, the Agreement on Technical Barriers to Trade, the Agreement on Customs Valuations, or rules of origin; while services are subject to the GATS. The underlying differences between agreements and the resulting implications for domestic policies have been the main factors in countries' favouring specific proposals. For example, the European Communities has proposed that all electronic transmissions be classified as services (WTO 1999a),[10] which would be subject to the GATS.

This would (among other things) allow the EU to restrict the imports of audio-visual services (including television programmes and movies). The United States, on the other hand, leans towards a "goods classification" or GATT approach, arguing that this "could provide for a more trade liberalizing outcome for electronic commerce" (WTO, 1999f). A similar controversy between the United States and the EU is taking place in the discussion on Internet taxation (see section III).

In general, the multilateral rules for services are still far less elaborate than the multilateral rules for trade in goods, providing countries with substantially more leeway for national policy discretion in the services trade. One important difference between the GATT and the GATS relates to general obligations. While the GATT's general obligations include most-favoured-nation treatment (MFN), national treatment and a general prohibition on quantitative restrictions, the GATS includes the national treatment principle only in negotiated specific commitments and specific services. For example, WTO member countries have defined in their national schedules whether, for a certain services trade, foreign suppliers will be given national treatment, i.e. whether they are subject to the same rules as domestic suppliers of the equivalent service. In other words, if a country grants national treatment, and if the WTO Members decide to include electronic transmissions in the GATS framework, no additional taxes can be imposed on foreign suppliers by that country. If no national treatment is specified, on the other hand, imports could be subject to higher taxes than domestically supplied services.

A second important difference between the GATS and the GATT is the possibility of imposing quantitative restrictions or quotas.

---

[10] This corresponds to an EU proposal on Internet taxation, which suggests that, for consumption tax purposes, trade in digitized goods should be treated as a supply of services (European Commission, 1999, 2000).

While the GATT (in general) prohibits the use of quotas, they are allowed under the GATS (depending on the market access commitment specified in a country's schedule). Theoretically, therefore, this could mean that a country could put (in principle) a limit on, say, the number of books transmitted electronically via the Internet.[11]

The question therefore remains, to what extent are e-commerce-related services covered by individual countries' national schedules? It would be important for countries to review their schedules with respect to the supply of electronic services before the next round of services negotiations. In particular, developing countries should identify those services sectors where they have a comparative advantage in the export of electronic services.

It becomes clear from the above discussion that the classification question has wide implications for the electronic trade of goods and services and therefore for the organization of production and distribution, which relate directly to the underlying rules of the existing multilateral agreements. Border tariffs are one of the problems to be addressed, especially given their potential impact on government revenue. Should electronic transmissions be defined as services and thus tariff-exempted, fiscal losses would occur. In addition, most imported goods are subject to domestic taxation, which in the case of services is usually lower or non-existing. Should these goods now be imported electronically and be tax-exempted because they are classified as services, further revenue losses would occur. The following section moves to the debate on taxation and e-commerce and looks at how tax revenues may be affected by e-commerce.

---

[11] Although it is not clear how this could be enforced, it is a question that has to be solved in the discussions on how to include e-commerce in the WTO agreements.

II.   E-COMMERCE TAXATION

Contrary to the debate on customs duties, where a number of countries have advocated a "tariff-free" environment, nobody has so far proposed that e-commerce be made "tax-free". Rather, it should be "tax-neutral" or subject to the same taxation as conventional commerce. Furthermore, the taxation debate clearly moves beyond goods or digitized products and includes traditional services, which are subject to consumption taxes in many countries.

The main players in the debate on e-commerce taxation have been the United States, the EU and the OECD.[12] The United States and the EU member States are primarily concerned with how their respective tax systems will be affected by e-commerce.[13] The OECD secretariat, whose Model Tax Convention serves as a basis for most bilateral tax treaties (including between non-OECD member countries), has been asked by its member States to take the international leadership role on e-commerce and taxation, a mandate that was confirmed at the 1998 OECD Ministerial Meeting in Ottawa. It has prepared a number of taxation principles that should govern e-commerce and has worked closely with the EU on consumption tax issues.

Developing countries have participated little in these debates and the proposals and papers so far produced by the OECD countries have given little consideration to developing countries' concerns.[14] While it is true that developing countries' shares in e-commerce are still modest, the international rules and regulations that are adopted now will impact on e-commerce in many countries in the future, including in the developing countries. In addition, the increasing number of small and medium-sized enterprises (SMEs) that will be drawn in by e-commerce from the developing countries have little experience in international taxation issues. It is therefore crucial to include their concerns as early as possible. This section will briefly introduce two key issues currently debated as regards Internet taxation (besides customs tariffs): consumption taxes and income taxes. It will present proposals that have been put forward on how to change existing tax regulation in the light of e-commerce and discuss possible implications for developing countries.

---

[12] Business as well as government institutions have participated in these debates and made proposals on how to handle Internet-related tax questions. While business interests are less of a concern in this paper, it should be noted that they mainly relate to avoiding double taxation and to simplifying indirect taxation that arises from inconsistencies among definitions, classification, source of supply rules for services, registration requirements, reverse charges, collection etc. For further discussion, see Global Information Infrastructure Commission (GIIC) website at www.gii.org.

[13] In 1998, the United States Congress created the Advisory Commission on Electronic Commerce under the Internet Tax Freedom Act, to study a variety of issues involving e-commerce taxation, including international issues. The Commission is collecting proposals from the public and private sectors for consideration, which will contribute to the final report and recommendations it will provide to Congress no later than April 2001. At its final meeting in March 2000 (Dallas, Texas), the Commission voted, among others, to extend a three-year moratorium on domestic "new" Internet taxation imposed by the Internet Tax Freedom Act and due to expire at the end of 2000. However, no solutions have yet been provided on the question of state and local tax collection, a major concern to local governments. Within the EU, various bodies have addressed and prepared background documents on Internet taxation (e.g. the EU's Taxation Policy Group, the EC Directorate-General on Taxation and Customs Union).

[14] An earlier OECD proposal on basic principles of international e-commerce taxation made reference to developing countries, stating that "any tax arrangements adopted domestically and any changes to existing international tax principles should be structured to ensure a fair sharing of the Internet tax base between countries, particularly important as regards division of the tax base between developed and developing countries" (Owen, 1997). However, this principle was not included in the final set of basic principles agreed upon in 1998 (OECD, 1998a).

A. Consumption taxes

The erosion of the consumption tax base resulting from e-commerce has caused considerable concern among Governments, given the steep growth of e-commerce in the past years and predictions for the next five years.

Consumption taxes usually include value-added taxes, sales taxes and turnover taxes. Traditionally, they are borne by the consumer and collected by the seller; different rules apply depending on the product or service sold, the location of consumer and seller, and the type of consumer (business or individual). With e-commerce, the number of foreign on-line suppliers, who are often subject to different taxation rules, has increased considerably. Research carried out in the United States on the impact of taxation on Internet commerce and consumer on-line purchasing patterns found that consumers living in high sales tax areas are significantly more likely to buy on-line than those living in low sales tax areas (Goolsbee, 1999). Hence, differentiated Internet taxation rules among countries could have a significant impact on consumers' purchasing behaviour, shifting from domestic to foreign suppliers.[15]

This raises several problems for tax authorities. First, it leads to the gradual elimination of intermediaries (so-called disintermediation) such as wholesalers or local retailers, who in the past have been critical for identifying taxpayers, especially private consumers. Second, foreign suppliers may be tax-exempted, whereas local suppliers are normally required to charge value added tax (VAT) or sales taxes. Third, direct orders from foreign suppliers could substantially increase the number of low-value shipments of physical goods to individual customers. These low-value packages now fall under so-called *de minimis* relief from customs duties and taxes in many countries, basically to balance the cost of collection and the amount of tax due. A substantial increase in these shipments as a result of e-commerce (where foreign suppliers replace domestic ones) could pose an additional challenge to tax as well as customs authorities.

Major differences exist between the EU and the United States in the way taxes are redeemed and hence in their approaches to international taxation rules on e-commerce. The EU countries derive a large proportion of government tax revenue from taxes on domestic goods and services (mainly VAT) (29 per cent, see Table 1). In addition, VAT extra charges contribute 45 per cent to the EU Community budget (in addition to customs duties and GNP contributions).[16] Their main concern is the increasing import of digital content and services from outside the EU, which would be exempted from VAT payments in the EU. The United States Government, on the other hand, derives most of its tax revenues from personal and corporate income tax and social security contributions; revenues from taxes on domestic goods and services are extremely low (3.6 per cent).[17] The United States is currently both a net exporter and the main exporter of e-commerce worldwide. Hence, it has a great interest in encouraging business (including e-commerce business) to locate in the United

---

[15] Although there are also barriers that could prevent this shift, such as other regulatory obstacles (besides taxation), delivery problems, or cultural and linguistic barriers. To circumvent these, some United States suppliers have started to buy local competitors in Europe (The Economist, 2000b).

[16] The 45 per cent contribution in 1997 (the date of Table 1) was reduced to 35 per cent in 1999 (projection) (European Commission, 1998).

[17] Within the United States, individual states and local governments have autonomy over determining and collecting state and local sales tax, often their biggest source of revenue. Sales taxes differ substantially among states, ranging from 0 to 7 per cent. United States-based on-line suppliers selling to out-of-state (including foreign) customers do currently not have to charge local sales tax. States are therefore becoming increasingly worried about how to secure their sales tax revenues in the light of Internet commerce.

States and pay direct taxes to United States tax authorities.

Therefore, the issue of consumption taxes has received most attention in the OECD and the EU. In particular, the EU feels very strongly about maintaining VAT duties and is likely to modify tax rules in a way that will ensure a continuation of VAT contributions, rather than lowering or eliminating them. A closer look at current VAT regulations in the EU will explain the growing concern among EU tax authorities and Governments.[18]

Goods. Imported goods from non-EU members are subject to (import duties and) VAT of the importing country. Sales within the EU are subject to the VAT of the receiving country in the case of business-to-consumer trade. Businesses selling to businesses in another member State are tax-exempted; the receiving or importing business is required to pay VAT locally (i.e. in the country of final consumption).[19] Exports to non-EU countries are zero-rated.

Services. Services differ according to the type of services traded. In the case of information (currently the majority of e-services), imports from non-EU businesses to EU consumers are not subject to customs duties and are VAT-exempted (except for Denmark, France and Italy). Sales from non-EU businesses to EU businesses are subject to self-accounted VAT at the local rate (a so-called reverse charge). Intra-EU service suppliers are required to charge VAT in the country in which they are established (location of the seller), if selling to private

consumers. EU-business-to-business services trade is subject to VAT in the country of the final consumer. Sales to customers outside the EU are subject to VAT in the location of the seller (European Commission, 1999; Kerrigan, 1999).

The challenges to EU tax authorities that arise from e-commerce therefore lie in non-EU supplies of e-services to EU customers (and in an increase in non-EU customers not subject to EU VAT). Under current tax law, these are exempted from VAT, while at the same time their share is increasing, in direct competition with EU suppliers who are subject to VAT payments. Furthermore, the VAT exemption provides incentives for suppliers to locate outside the EU, a fairly easy undertaking in e-commerce, which no longer requires the presence of human and technical resources.

A number of suggestions have been made on how to modify and harmonize VAT legislation in order to accommodate e-commerce. The OECD has come up with "framework conditions" on consumption taxes, recommending that (OECD, 1998a):

- The taxation of cross-border trade should be in the jurisdiction where the consumption takes place;

- The supply of digitized products should not be treated as a supply of goods for consumption tax purposes (differences in the definition among countries may lead to uncertainties about the tax treatment of products from outside suppliers);

- Where services and intangible property (i.e. goods) from suppliers outside the country are acquired, countries should examine the use of reverse charge, self-assessment or other equivalent mechanisms;

- Appropriate systems should be developed to collect tax on the importation of physical goods.

---

[18] For details and facts on EU VAT rules, see European Commission (1997). The complexity of the existing EU VAT system is considered by business a major barrier to developing e-commerce in Europe.

[19] This regulation was put in place in 1993 under the "transitional VAT arrangements", with the objective of removing border controls for tax purposes inside the European Community.

The first two recommendations deserve further consideration. Since it is unlikely that non-EU sellers will collect taxes from their EU customers for EU tax authorities (or any foreign supplier for another country's tax authorities), it seems reasonable to move VAT collection to the place of consumption, away from the location of the seller.[20] Here, a key problem for tax authorities will be to identify the customer and the location of the jurisdiction responsible for collecting the tax. Because of the process of disintermediation, apart from the seller and the customer there are no other parties involved in the transactions (which could collect the tax). Credit card companies, Internet service providers (ISPs), banking and payment systems providers or telecommunications companies have been mentioned as potential new intermediaries in verifying the location of a customer and the respective tax jurisdiction. This, of course, raises privacy issues and possible abuses of information. It could also lead to an increasing use of foreign credit cards or digital cash; needless to say, the customer's location may differ from the billing address. In addition, how can an Internet seller determine whether the customer is a business or an individual consumer, each of which is subject to different VAT rules? An increasing number of e-commerce businesses are small entrepreneurs operating from home who may receive services for business or personal purposes.

The OECD proposal to treat digitized products as services corresponds to an EU proposal that for VAT purposes trade in digital goods be treated as a supply of services. The EU also proposes that VAT rates on all e-services be harmonized into a single rate. This could result in tax losses since consumption taxes are lower on services than on goods. It could also lead to losses on tariffs and import duties on digital goods that were shipped physically in the past and which would now be subject to much lower duties. This would impact in particular on the developing countries, whose reliance on import duties as a government revenue source is much higher than in the developed countries (Table 1). Data on potential revenue losses, if digitized products were exempted from import duties and taxes, are presented in the next section.

At the Ottawa Conference, the United States took a different position on this issue: digital products should be characterized on the basis of the "rights transferred" in each particular case. It argued that some goods which are now zero-rated (such as books or newspapers) would be subject to VAT if treated as a service. Customers may therefore prefer to buy local zero-rated books rather than digitally imported (and taxed) services, many of which could be supplied by United States on-line providers.

As an alternative, the United States has proposed an origin-based consumption tax for intangibles (e-services), which would be collected from the supplier and not from the consumer. It argues that it is easier to identify the supplier than the customer on the basis of permanent establishment rule (see below) and since businesses are subject to audit. The United States as a net exporter of e-commerce would benefit from an origin-based tax, while it may further erode the tax base in e-commerce-importing countries. On the other hand, it disadvantages domestic producers in their export sales since they would have to pay the tax on the exports, instead of the final consumer. This may encourage business to set up shop in countries with no origin-based taxation. Finally, one needs to keep in mind that most e-commerce will be business-to-business (currently 80 per cent of e-commerce), which is often tax-exempted or

---

[20] The EU has proposed that non-EU suppliers selling in the EU be required to apply taxes on the same basis as an EU operator when transacting business in the EU. In order to facilitate compliance, they propose that non-EU e-commerce operators be required to register in one EU member State and have the possibility of discharging all their obligations by dealing with a single tax administration (European Commission, 2000).

subject to voluntary compliance.[21]

How does consumption tax legislation affect developing countries? Most of them rely heavily on consumption taxes for their government budgets (Table 1). Given that many developing countries will be net importers of e-commerce in the medium term, they would have a strong interest in not eroding their tax bases by switching to an origin-based tax system. They need to be aware, however, that tax collection on e-commerce activities will require access to the latest technologies by tax authorities. Thus, developing countries need to catch up on modernizing their tax administration systems in order not to lose important tax revenues on the collection of consumption taxes.

To avoid double taxation, some multi- or bilateral agreements have to be adopted on where consumption taxes are to be collected: in the country where the supplier is established, the country where the customer is established or the country of consumption. A proposal by the EU to require non-EU suppliers to register for and charge VAT in a EU country would not favour providers from developing countries, thus placing an additional burden on their e-commerce exports.

B.   Income taxes

The taxation of income, profits and capital gains is another major source of government revenue, especially in the developed countries. There are two basic concepts of how countries tax income.   First, source-based taxation is applied in the jurisdiction where the economic activity takes place, for example the sale of the service or digital good traded. Foreigners who do not reside in the jurisdiction where their economic activity takes place are still taxed on their profits earned in that jurisdiction. Second, residence-based taxation takes place in the jurisdiction of place of residence of the person/business earning the income. In other words, taxpayers are taxed on their worldwide income by the country in which they live. Among the OECD countries, it is agreed that if a "permanent establishment" has been determined, source-based taxation applies; if not, residence-based tax principles apply (Lukas, 1999). The usual practice among OECD countries is to tax residents on their worldwide income and non-residents on the income they earn in the relevant country.[22] To avoid double taxation, countries enter into bilateral treaties, for example to reduce or eliminate source tax. Treaties are normally based on the OECD Model Tax Convention, which defines residence-based taxation according to where the management takes place. If no treaty exists, domestic tax legislation governs the taxation of non-resident businesses carrying on business in the country. In this case, the source principles generally apply.

Traditionally, direct taxation of income has used the "permanent establishment principle" used in the OECD Model Tax Convention (Article 5) to determine in which country income has been generated and is therefore taxed. Accordingly, business profits of non-resident enterprises may only be taxed in a country to the extent that they are attributable to a permanent establishment that the enterprise has in that country, which must also be a "fixed place of

---

[21] Recent predictions give business-to-consumer e-commerce steep growth rates as well.   According to Forrester Research, business-to-consumer e-commerce in the United States accounted for US$ 20 billion in 1999, and is expected to reach US$ 184 billion by 2004. Goldman-Sachs estimates that electronic shopping could account for 15-20 per cent by 2010 (The Economist, 2000b).

[22] The United States is again a different case: United States citizens are subject to taxation on their total global income in the United States, no matter whether they are resident in the United States or in another country. United States taxation law allows them, however, to offset the taxes paid in their country of residence against their United States tax liability.

business". However, the principle was drafted in 1963 and is not fully compatible with e-commerce as it relies on physical presence. For example, the source-based concept of income taxation could lead to a substantial erosion of the tax base since the link between income-generating activity and a specific location becomes blurred in e-commerce. In particular, the question of whether a website or web server can constitute a permanent establishment or fixed place of business has been at the centre of the debate. The OECD has therefore proposed the following amendments to Article 5, which would be applied to e-commerce (OECD, 2000):

- An Internet website does not constitute a "place of business", as there is "no facility such as premises or, in certain circumstances, machinery or equipment". On the other hand, the server operating the website is a piece of equipment which needs a physical location and may thus constitute a "fixed place of business" of the enterprise that operates it.

- A distinction between the enterprise that operates the server and the enterprise that carries on business through the website is necessary. If the website is hosted by an Internet Service Provider (ISP) and a different enterprise carries on business through the website, the server cannot be considered a fixed place of business. The server and its location are not at the disposal of the enterprise and the enterprise does not have a physical presence in that place since the website does not involve tangible assets.

- A server constitutes a "fixed" place of business if it is located in a certain place for a sufficient period of time.

- In the case of ISPs, even though they own and operate the servers (i.e. fixed place of business), they cannot be considered to constitute permanent establishments of the businesses whose websites they host, because they will not have the authority to conclude contracts in the name of the enterprises they

host and thus are not agents of those enterprises.

- Whether computer equipment used for e-commerce operations may be considered permanent establishment needs to be examined on a case-by-case basis, depending on whether the equipment is used for activities that form an essential part of the commercial activity of an enterprise (as opposed to being used for merely preparatory or auxiliary activities). In this case, and if the equipment constitutes a fixed place of business, it would be a permanent establishment of the enterprise.[23]

What would be possible implications for tax revenues if these amendments to Article 5 were implemented? For example, if a web server would constitute a permanent establishment of a business, and since little resources are needed to set up and maintain a server, it could encourage the migration of servers and computer equipment to low-tax countries, including some of the developing countries. Currently, the United States has the highest concentration of web servers in the world;[24] should these be considered permanent establishments and thus be subject to direct taxation, the United States may take a minimalist position on income tax to prevent servers from migrating across the border. One problem that needs to be addressed is tracing the legal entity operating a business through a website and identifying the business and its physical location.

Because of the difficulties in defining permanent establishment (and because of its large tax base), the United States has favoured residence-based taxation over source-based taxation. However, residence-based taxation may

---

[23] OECD member countries have not yet agreed on what "core functions" of an enterprise could be.

[24] According to *The Economist* (2000b), the United States currently accounts for 90 per cent of commercial websites.

13

not favour developing countries, given their small number of residents with e-businesses. In the short run, they are primarily net e-commerce importing countries; hence, they would have an interest in source-based rather than residence-based taxation. Also, a move to residence-based taxation may shift tax revenues from developing to developed countries once developing countries' share as consumers of e-commerce increases. On the other hand, residence-based taxation favours tax havens, often developing countries. Here, developing countries could be attractive to foreign investors looking for certain, low-skilled activities in the production of digital content.

If Article 5 is not amended, countries that are net importers of technology may face significant revenue losses because businesses may close down branches and replace them with Internet communications and e-commerce, which would not be regarded as permanent establishments and would thus be tax-free. Hence, the main business activity would not take place in the country any more, and the country's source-based tax would decrease.

C. A need for global coordination

No matter what changes to existing tax legislation are adopted, without a certain degree of international cooperation and harmonization of existing tax rules, the expansion of e-commerce will be hampered. Traditionally, tax collection has been based on the belief that individual countries have the right to set their own tax rules and little international cooperation and few multilateral agreements have been put in place. Unless this approach changes and countries agree to enter into multilateral tax agreements, tax competition will intensify with e-commerce. This is a likely scenario given that, even within the OECD, individual countries implement domestic tax rules that give them a

competitive edge.[25] This is also why it is unlikely that countries will collect taxes for other countries, for example in the case of VAT, where it has been suggested that VAT be collected from the country of the supplier (The Economist, 2000b). On the other hand, if rules are not harmonized internationally, the risk of double taxation may keep foreign suppliers/competition out; and non-taxation may distort competition against local suppliers.

With a few exceptions, developing countries will not be part of an OECD agreement on Internet taxation. Nevertheless, they can use the principles and rules agreed upon as a basis for adjusting their own legislation. For example, developing countries have used tax legislation in the past to attract private foreign direct investment (FDI). Multinationals increasingly operate in countries that have low taxes or are willing to negotiate favourable tax regimes to attract foreign business (The Economist, 2000b). In fact, fiscal incentives are the most widely used type of FDI incentives (UNCTAD, 1996). Depending on the agreements adopted in the OECD, developing countries could negotiate specific bilateral treaties for e-commerce taxation, which would give them a competitive edge. For example, the transaction costs of setting up or moving a web server are low; hence, e-commerce allows companies to respond quickly to tax incentives by Governments and move their web servers to a developing country.

Any decisions which developing countries may take on modifying their tax legislation to accommodate e-commerce, however, will have to take into account the significant role of tax and tariff revenues in their national budgets. Until new international agreements on e-commerce taxation have been defined, an increasing number of goods and services will be traded on-line, largely tax-free. This will have an effect on

_____

[25] And even within the EU, VAT differs among member states.

government revenue, especially if the goods and services have been subject to import duties in the past. In order to capture some of these (potential) revenue losses, the following section will analyze data on trade, tariffs and other import duties for a number of goods that are already supplied on-line or are likely to be so in the near future.

III. TRADE AND TARIFF REVENUES ON DIGITIZABLE PRODUCTS

Until WTO member States have agreed on whether electronic transmissions should be classified as goods or services, discussions will continue on the question of potential tariff revenue losses resulting from a ban on customs duties. As a contribution to this debate, this section will analyze trade and tariff data for goods possibly concerned by the ban. It will provide detailed information on tariff revenues currently obtained from imports of these goods, in particular for developing countries.

For this purpose, a number of commodities have been selected, which traditionally fall under an importation and are thus dutiable, but which today can be transformed into a digitized format and sent through the Internet. More specifically, these "digitizable products" (DP) are here defined as goods, identifiable by HS headings, that can be sent both physically via a carrier medium and electronically via networks. They include five product categories: (i) printed matter, (ii) software, (iii) music and other media, (iv) film, and (v) video games. Table 2 shows the corresponding HS96 headings for each category and subcategory.[26]

Some of these products are already traded electronically, albeit on a small scale. For example, software products can be purchased and downloaded from the Internet. New technology allows music to be digitized, downloaded (often free-of-charge) from the Internet onto a PC, a CD or a new portable carrier medium that allows storing, deleting and listening to music now in digitized format.[27] Newspapers and journals have long been offered on the Internet. A number of on-line bookstores have started to offer "electronic books", which can be delivered through the Internet and read off-line on special, portable electronic book readers. These are but a few examples indicating the future directions for the distribution of traditional goods through e-commerce. Currently, these transactions are largely at the retail or business-to-consumer level, and little electronic distribution is taking place among businesses.[28] Therefore, its use is limited to consumers or individual customers with Internet access. One could well imagine, however, the content of some of the products considered here being shipped electronically to national distributors where it would be put on a carrier medium and domestically sold. For some products, such as software, this could already be the case in the near future; others such as film, where the video quality for broadband still needs to be improved, will take longer. Much will also depend on careful consideration of all costs involved, including transportation, production and distribution costs.[29]

Another important aspect relevant to this discussion is the speed with which these changes

---

[26] The HS96 coding system was chosen over the Standard International Trade Classification (SITC) coding system since it provides for the identification of software, an important product in this group (neither the previous SITC nor the HS88 coding system has a heading that corresponds to software products). A proposal to introduce in the next version of the HS system, to be released in 2002, three new codes that would specifically define software products was rejected owing to a disagreement among WCO members.

[27] Currently, the most common technology in digitized audio is called "MP3". Music that has been digitized into MP3 format can be downloaded from the Internet onto portable digital audio players (MP3 players). See numerous Internet sites for further information.

[28] To be sure, the large majority of today's e-commerce activities (estimates range from 70 to 85 per cent of the total) are taking place among businesses. These include mostly services-related activities. In contrast, this and the following section refer to the on-line distribution of a limited number of products which can be shipped either physically or electronically. Currently, this distribution is largely taking place on a business-to-customer basis. For an analysis of business-to-business e-commerce see OECD (1999a).

[29] For a discussion on the economics of e-commerce, see Panagariya (2000) and The Economist (2000a).

will take place. While in the United States – and closely followed by Europe – e-commerce is growing rapidly, it will take much longer for many developing countries to have access to the necessary infrastructure to take advantage of e-commerce.[30]

A. World trade in digitizable products

The most important exporter of digitizable products is the United States, accounting for almost 20 per cent of world exports (Table 3). It is followed by the United Kingdom, Germany, Ireland, Japan, France and Netherlands, which combined account for 66.5 per cent of total exports. Developed countries[31] account for 91 per cent of exports, while the developing countries' share is only 9 per cent. Data show that developed countries account for above-average shares in all the product categories identified here; their highest share is, however, in the export of software products (95 per cent of all exports). Among the developing countries, the main exporters of digitizable products are Singapore, Hong Kong (China), China, Mexico, the Republic of Korea, India, Honduras and Chile.

On the import side, the United States has again the largest share accounting for 16 per cent of all imports, followed by the United Kingdom, Canada, Germany, France, Japan, Switzerland and the Netherlands. The developing countries' share is 16 per cent (i.e. 84 per cent for the developed countries). The main importers among the developing countries include Hong Kong (China), Mexico, the Republic of Korea, China, Singapore, Brazil, South Africa, India and Argentina.

Growth rates[32] for both exports and imports of digitized products are significantly higher than growth rates for total merchandise trade. In particular, developing countries' imports have grown considerably throughout the decade, although they slowed down in 1997 and 1998 (Table 4).

The diverse nature of products included here, and the way they are differently impacted by technological advancement (and therefore potential delivery over the Internet), suggest a further breakdown of the analysis. Tables 5, 6, 7 and Figures 2 and 3 show more detailed information on export and import shares of each of the five product categories identified here. For example, printed matter takes the largest share in digitizable goods trade (54 per cent), followed by software (20 per cent), sound and media (17 per cent), video games (7 per cent) and film (2 per cent). A few observations can be made.

1. Exports of digitizable products

- Film exports (including both photographic and cinematographic film, with the latter having the larger share) are the only e-commerce product group where the export shares of developed and developing countries correspond to their shares in total world merchandise exports (i.e. 79 per cent for developed countries, 11 per cent for developing countries). However, total trade in these products is fairly small and accounts for only 2 per cent of trade in digitizable products.

- Developing countries' export shares are particularly small in sound and media

---

[30] For a discussion on developing countries' participation in e-commerce, see UNCTAD (1998).

[31] In this paper, countries with economies in transition have been included in the "developed country" group.

[32] The HS96 system only provides trade data from 1996 onwards. For the calculation of annual growth rates at the aggregated level, HS88 headings were used. At the (disaggregated) five-category level no time-series analysis was possible.

products, software and video games; they have slightly higher shares in the export of film and printed matter.

- Two countries – Ireland and the Unites States – account for almost 60 per cent of software product exports. They are followed by other members of the European Union. Among the major developing country exporters are Singapore (in seventh position among world exporters), the Republic of Korea (in twenty-second position), Hong Kong (China), Malaysia, China and Chile.[33]

- A total of 55 per cent of world exports of video games are supplied by Japan.

2. Imports of digitizable products

- Developing countries' import shares of film products are higher than those of the other digitizable products (21 per cent compared with 15 per cent of all digitizable products).

- Developing countries' software imports are much higher than their exports: 12 per cent compared with 5 per cent.

- A total of 83 per cent of world imports of video games go to the United States; developing countries' shares of imports of this product account for only 6 per cent.

To summarize the results from data on trade flows of digitizable goods, the following points can be made. First, trade flows vary considerably among products in terms of quantity, origin and

destination. Second, a few developed countries largely dominate trade in digitizable products, particularly on the export side. For most of these countries, trade in digitizable goods (DG) amounts to about 1 per cent of total trade, although figures go as high as 14 per cent. Available growth rates suggest, however, that these numbers may change rapidly, including for the developing countries.[34] Finally, developing countries' shares as importers and exporters differ according to specific products; in goods that require higher levels of technology and know-how, such as software or video games, their export shares are rather low, whereas in areas such as books, newspapers, film and music disks their shares are higher.

Bearing in mind the main objective of the study, these trade flows now have to be linked to tariff rates currently imposed on the various products. This will help calculate potential revenue losses resulting from a shift from physical to electronic delivery of goods.

B. Tariff rates on digitizable goods

Table 8 provides an overview of applied MFN tariff rates for digitizable products per country. It compares both average and import-weighted MFN rates. While the former amounts to 11.6 per cent for all countries, the latter is 7 per cent. The tariff rates of the developing countries are higher than those of developed countries. The ten countries levying the highest tariff rates on digitizable products are Bangladesh, India, Pakistan, the Solomon Islands, Egypt, Burkina Faso, Morocco, Tunisia, Congo, and Thailand.

While this is useful for ascertaining which countries might be most affected by a ban on customs duties on these goods (in the event of replacement of physical by electronic delivery),

---

[33] It may come as a surprise that India is not among the main developing country software exporters. This can be explained by the structure of the Indian software industry where software *services* account for 95 per cent of Indian exports, whereas software *packages* (i.e. the products considered here) constitute only a small proportion of the Indian software industry output (Heeks, 1998).

---

[34] See also Schuknecht (1999).

it does not offer much information on the tariff rates levied on different products. This is important, however, for any further negotiations on these products. It also plays an important role considering that not all products are likely to be replaced immediately or in the near future, and some may always be distributed in physical or "tangible" format.

Table 9 and Figure 4 show average applied MFN tariff rates per product line and product category, and Table 10 shows tariffs per product grouping and country. Significant differences exist among the products. For example, while low tariffs (2-3 per cent) prevail on books and newspapers, high tariffs (up to 20 per cent) are imposed on postcards, calendars and commercial catalogues – all of which comprise the "printed matter" group. Higher tariffs also dominate most of the sound and media products as well as video games. A disaggregation of the average MFN tariff by developed/developing country shows that developing countries on the average have higher tariffs on all product lines compared with developed countries. As can be seen in the next section, this has major implications for their tariff revenues resulting from imports of these goods.

It should be noted that the tables do not take into consideration specific tariffs (i.e. not *ad valorem* rates) imposed on the import of certain goods. Specific tariffs are measured per unit of import rather than by their value. Given the lack of information on volumes per product line, they could not be included here. Specific tariffs usually imply a somewhat higher rate of protection than simple *ad valorem* rates. Imports of digitized goods falling under specific duties amount to 18 per cent of world imports for sound and media, 16 per cent for software, 10 per cent for film, 7 per cent for printed matter and 1 per cent for video games. The main countries (or territories) imposing specific tariffs are the following:

Film:	EU (cine film), Switzerland,[35] Republic of Korea, Taiwan
Printed matter:	Switzerland, United States, Nigeria, Panama
Software:	United States, Switzerland, Panama
Sound/media:	United States, Switzerland, Japan
Video games:	Switzerland, Panama

C.   Tariff revenues

What fiscal losses would occur should physical delivery of products be replaced by electronic delivery and no tariffs imposed on the latter? Tables 9 and 11 (and Figure 5) show fiscal losses per product grouping and per country. The calculation is based on weighted average applied MFN rates.[36]

The data show that the majority of countries most affected by tariff revenue losses come from the developing world. Given their higher levels of MFN rates, this should not come as a surprise. What is remarkable, however, is the magnitude: despite the developing countries' import share in digitizable products of only 16 per cent (see Table 3), their *absolute* tariff revenue (loss) is almost double that of the developed countries, amounting to 63 per cent of world tariff revenue losses for these products (Figure 6). This clearly shows that, as far as potential fiscal losses are concerned, developing countries would be much more affected by the proposed ban. The ten countries most affected by fiscal loss are the EU, India, Canada, Mexico, Brazil, China, the Russian Federation, Poland, Argentina and Thailand.

---

[35] Switzerland imposes specific rates on all non-zero-rated imports (all products).

[36] Applied rates are averaged at the 6-digit level; rates are import-weighted at the aggregate level (2- or 4-digit level).

Despite relatively lower tariff rates, highest losses occur in the product categories of printed matter (books, commercial catalogues, cards), but also in software products, disks and CDs, owing to the higher trade values of these products.

The countries mainly affected by fiscal losses according to product category are:

Film: EU, Russian Federation, Mexico, United States, Canada

Printed matter: Canada, Mexico, EU, India, China

Software: India, Brazil, Canada, Malaysia, Poland

Sound/media: EU, Brazil, Canada, India, Mexico

Videogames: EU, China, Paraguay, Russian Federation, Mexico

These losses now need to be placed in the context of total government revenues. Table 11 compares tariff revenues from digitizable products with total revenues and revenues from import duties. As has been shown elsewhere (Schuknecht, 1999), the percentages are relatively low: for all countries, tariff revenues from these products amount to only 0.06 per cent of total government revenues and 0.9 per cent of revenues from import duties. Nevertheless, some significant differences exist between countries, with shares ranging from 0 to 0.7 per cent of total revenue and from 0 to 6 per cent of revenues from import duties. Furthermore, as has been shown in Table 1, customs duties as a source of government revenue play a much more important role in a number of developing countries: while government revenues from import duties account for 2.6 per cent in developed countries, they account for 15.8 per cent in the developing countries.

The data also show that while developing countries' tariff revenues from digitizable products are higher than developed countries' as a share of total government revenues, as a share

of import duties they are in fact lower. This suggests that on average developed countries impose higher tariffs on digitizable products than on other products, compared with developing countries.

D.   Implications of the Information Technology Agreement

At the first WTO Ministerial Conference in Singapore (1996), 29 countries signed the Declaration on Trade in Information Technology Products, often referred to as the Information Technology Agreement (ITA). The ITA came into effect on 1 April 1997 and by the end of 1999 the number of signatories had increased to 48 (including 15 EU member States), covering approximately 90 per cent of world trade in information technology products. It calls for the elimination of customs duties on a wide range of information-technology-related products. Customs duties were supposed to be eliminated gradually, with a completion date of 1 January 2000. A number of countries have asked for an extension of the period until, at the latest, 2005.

Some of the products considered here (largely software products) are covered by the ITA. Therefore, the question arises as to what will happen to import revenues if these products, which were previously subject to import tariffs, are zero-rated. Table 12 lists all countries that are both included in this study and ITA signatories, and shows tariff revenues before eliminating tariffs on digitizable products covered by the ITA.[37] Accordingly, tariff revenues would be

---

[37]   The ITA also requires countries to eliminate "additional import duties" on the products concerned (see following section). Although these are not specifically defined, it is assumed here that they include all additional surcharges except internal taxes. The large majority of signatories do not impose additional duties on these products (although all impose internal taxes on their imports), with the exception of India, Israel, the Kyrgyzstan, Latvia, Panama and Taiwan Province of China. No calculations were therefore made on the amount

reduced by 27 per cent for all countries, and by 18 per cent for the developing countries. The countries mostly affected are those of the EU, India, Canada, Malaysia, Poland and the Republic of Korea.

---

of additional duties.

IV.   ADDITIONAL IMPORT DUTIES AND TAXES

The discussions on import duties and potential revenue losses that could result from a switch to electronic commerce have usually stopped here. However, apart from the applied tariffs, there are a number of additional duties and taxes levied on most imports by most countries, which also need to be taken into consideration. If imports of physical goods are replaced by electronic delivery that is exempted from customs duties, these additional duties would also be lost, besides the tariff duties. For most products, additional duties exceed tariff duties and hence could substantially change the revenue calculations presented in the previous section. They will be considered now.

A.   Types of additional duties and taxes

There are two types of additional duties levied on imports: (i) customs surcharges that are levied only on imports, and (ii) internal taxes that are levied on imports as well as on domestic goods. Importers are normally obliged to cover all of them. Customs surcharges usually consist of a mixture of duties, including undefined customs fees and uplifts or taxes such as statistical taxes, stamp taxes or port taxes. Internal taxes are usually value-added taxes, sales taxes or other types of consumption taxes. These additional duties could be levied on the import value (cost, insurance and freight (c.i.f.) or free on board (f.o.b.)) of the product, or on any combination of import value plus tariff plus other duties. Each country has its own regulations on how it levies and calculates import duties. Often, different types of products are subject to varying rates; for example, food products could be subject to reduced rates while luxury goods, tobacco or alcohol are often subject to increased rates.

B.   Calculation of additional duties

For the purposes of this paper, a database on additional duties levied on imports of digitizable products was created. While these duties do not differ substantially from duties levied on other imported products, some are characteristic of digitizable products: (i) books and printed matter are often exempted from consumption taxes; and (ii) most of the other digitizable products are subject to the "normal" rate levied on imports, hence no reduced and increased rates need to be taken into account.

A number of different sources were used for creating the database.[38] The data include all additional charges levied on imports of digitizable products that were reported in any of the sources. Key to the database is information on how the duties are calculated and on which products they are levied, including exemptions. The database also includes the MFN tariff rates and import values of digitizable products. The following methodology was applied for entering the data:

- Import values are based on partner country export data, which normally refer to f.o.b. values. Duties, however, are mostly levied on c.i.f. import values, which are somewhat higher. In addition, partner data are normally lower than real import data. It is estimated here that the partner values correspond to approximately 85-90 per cent of reported import values. Hence, the data on duties and revenues are likely to be somewhat higher than those calculated here.

- The information on import duties refers to the latest available years (1997 to 1999).

---

[38] Bureau of National Affairs, Inc. (various years), IFO Institute for Economic Research (1999), WTO (various years), KPMG (various years).

- In cases where no information was provided on the way taxes are levied (e.g. whether on import value, on import value plus tariff plus fees), the f.o.b. import value was taken as a basis.

- All exemptions were taken into consideration, i.e. either they were subtracted or, if applicable, the reduced rates were calculated. These largely concern VAT or sales taxes on books and other printed matter.

- The European Union member countries were treated differently, given the large share of intra-EU trade in world trade of digitizable products, which is tariff-exempted but not tax-exempted when crossing intra-EU borders. Therefore, EU trade has been separated into external and internal EU trade. While the external trade data were used to calculate tariff revenues and additional duties and taxes, the internal data were used to calculate the additional duties only (mainly VAT). It should be mentioned that each EU member country levies different VAT rates on the imports of goods (see section III).

- As mentioned before, some countries apply specific tariff rates (instead of *ad valorem* rates) to their imports. These could not be taken into consideration for calculating the tariff revenues. By contrast, values of imports subject to specific tariffs were able to be used to calculate additional duties, and these are included here.

C.   Amount of additional duties

How important are these duties compared with the tariff? How do they differ among countries and between developed and developing countries, given what we know about the differing tariff rates? Table 13 (and Figure 7) provides answers to these questions. Two key results should be highlighted.

First, compared with the tariff rates, the rates for additional duties are significantly higher. For all countries considered here (i.e. 120 countries), the additional duties and taxes levied on digitizable products amount on average to 23 per cent, compared with only 6.9 per cent for the tariff. The final calculation of the duties levied on imports therefore increases from 6.9 per cent (tariff only) to 29.2 per cent (tariff, customs surcharges, taxes).

Second, the amount of additional duties differs substantially among countries, ranging from 0 to 120 per cent. In the case of tariffs, the developing countries were clearly the ones imposing (on average) higher rates than the developed countries. In the case of other duties, however, the rates between developed and developing countries hardly differ; averages calculated here amount to 23.1 per cent for the former and 22.9 per cent for the latter. This is largely due to the relatively high consumption taxes charged by many (developing and developed) countries. They account for 15 per cent (all countries), 17.1 per cent (developed countries) and 14.3 per cent (developing countries). It confirms what was mentioned in the discussion on Internet taxation (section III): countries prefer to maintain a certain degree of autonomy over their domestic taxation legislation and use/change it in a way that gives them a competitive edge. Compared with the tariff rates, little has been accomplished at the international level to harmonize tax rates among countries, including import taxes.

Finally, the data show that customs surcharges (excluding consumption taxes) are higher in the developing countries (8.7 per cent) than in the developed countries (6.1 per cent).

D.   Revenues from customs duties and taxes

Given the relatively high rates of additional duties on imports of digitizable products, significant revenue increases resulting from these duties ought to be expected. Table 14, and Figures 8 and 9, compare tariff revenues, as calculated in the previous section, with revenues obtained from adding to the tariff the additional duties and taxes. The following can be observed.

First, the imbalance between the developed and developing countries, which we could observe from the tariff revenue data, has disappeared. This is largely due to the high consumption tax rates which developed countries levy on domestic goods and services (combined with their volume of trade in digitizable products). Shares now reflect the actual trade volumes of the products. Therefore, revenues resulting from duties and taxes are higher in the developed countries than in the developing countries.

Second, as far as absolute numbers are concerned, while revenues from tariff duties were almost double in the developing countries compared with the developed countries, revenues from all duties (tariffs, customs surcharges, taxes) are now much higher in the developed countries than in the developing countries: US$ 5.3 billion compared with US$ 1.3 billion for the developing countries. This amounts to a 78 per cent share of the developed countries' import duties resulting from digitizable products, compared with a 22 per cent share for the developing countries. The developing countries' share is still significantly higher than their share in world imports of these products (16 per cent for the latter; see Table 3). Again, a major explanation for these numbers is the consumption tax levied by the developed countries: revenues from these taxes amount to US$ 4.3 billion compared with US$ 647 million in the developing world.

Third, revenues from import duties and taxes on digitizable products now account on average for 0.3 per cent of total government revenue, up from 0.06 per cent (tariffs only). Their share in

tax revenues has increased from 0.08 per cent to 0.4 per cent. In both cases, this is an increase of 400 per cent. There is no major difference in these shares between developing and developed countries.

Fourth, shares in government import revenues have changed considerably. The combined tariff and customs surcharges (excluding consumption taxes) amount now to 2.8 per cent of total import revenue, up from 0.9 per cent (tariffs only), i.e. an increase of more than 300 per cent.

To summarize, it clearly emerges from the above data and discussion that fiscal losses resulting from replacing physical by digital products are substantially more than simple tariff revenue losses. Almost all countries levy some sort of additional duties and/or taxes on their imports, which normally exceed tariff duties. These revenues could be lost if goods were delivered digitally. The duties and taxes identified here are normally paid by the importer. In the case of on-line delivery, these intermediaries are likely to be eliminated and the product delivered directly to the final consumer. This could cause major problems in the area of tariff and tax collection, particularly if consumers are not registered businesses.

V. CONCLUSIONS

The main question addressed by this paper was how significant are fiscal losses from the non-collection of tariffs and taxes if e-commerce replaces traditional trade in goods, particularly for the developing countries. The analysis of trade and tariff data showed that while revenues from imports of digitizable products are small in absolute numbers and relative to total revenues, the developing countries' share in world tariff revenues from digitizable products is disproportionately higher than that of developed countries: while developing countries account for only 16 per cent of world imports of digitized goods, their share in tariff revenues resulting from these imports is 63 per cent. Developing countries would therefore be primarily concerned should physical delivery of goods be replaced by electronic delivery and tariffs not be collected.

Does this imply that they should reject a continuation of the proposed ban on customs duties? If there was no ban, would it have an impact on the growth of e-commerce in these products? The United States argument (strongly supported by the Alliance of Global Business) points to the symbolic nature of such an agreement: to free the Internet from duties will foster the expansion of e-commerce. One should keep in mind, however, that most e-commerce activities are currently dominated by United States businesses. And the proposed ban on customs duties (in its current form) does not address the question of whether to levy domestic and other taxes on electronic transactions.

From a developing country perspective, the immediate advantage of a ban is not clear. Although there is no immediate harm done to Governments' revenues, given that most of the goods concerned will continue to be traded physically in the short to medium term, making the ban binding and indefinite does not seem to be a precondition for the spread of e-commerce. Rather, from the developing country point of view, other issues that ensure the effective liberalization of e-commerce should have

priority. These include resolving the classification issue (i.e. the definition of electronic transmissions as goods, services or something else), identifying e-services in which developing countries have export potentials (such as software development, audiovisual products, data processing and tourism) and reviewing national commitments under GATS that concern e-services.

The relatively high tariffs imposed on some of the digitizable products need to be gradually reduced. Careful consideration needs to be given here to each product category; for example, a reduction on software products could support domestic investment in high-technology sectors, an important industry for helping developing countries participate in e-commerce. The Information Technology Agreement already covers some of the products that fall under software and media, and other products may and should be included in the near future.

The extension of the discussion on tariff revenues, to include additional import duties and taxes, considerably increases the amount of revenues collected from imports of digitizable products. Both customs surcharges and internal taxes levied on imports are significantly higher than the simple applied tariff rate. If these are not collected, and given the rapid growth rates of e-commerce, revenue losses could be felt in all countries.

In particular, the calculations of domestic taxes levied on imports demonstrated the significant impact e-commerce could have on tax revenues. In this study, only a small number of goods were considered, but the revenue impact is already considerable. If these calculations were extended to services, which are often subject to consumption taxes and which are the fastest growing e-business activities, the tax base of many countries could be substantially eroded.

The fiscal impact of international e-commerce is likely to be felt more strongly in the developing countries: they will face higher losses from customs duties, which make up higher shares in their national budgets compared with the developed countries. They will have less flexibility to replace those losses by shifting to other revenue sources, such as income taxes or social security contributions. In the short to medium term, developing countries will be net importers of e-commerce and hence will run a greater risk of losing tariff and tax revenues if traditional imports are replaced by on-line delivery. Therefore, the development of efficient tax collection systems for e-commerce should be a priority for all developing countries.

By looking at both tariff and tax revenues, the paper clearly showed that border tariff revenues are more important for the developing countries as a source of government revenue, while most developed countries' Governments depend primarily on income from VAT. In addition, developing countries often have difficulties in implementing an efficient VAT system. They would therefore be more affected by a cut in tariffs on electronic goods, while developed countries would be more affected by lost consumption taxes (an exception is the United States, which depends more on income taxes than on consumption taxes). This explains why, on the one hand, many OECD countries support the customs ban, while, on the other hand, they are particularly concerned with finding a solution to e-commerce taxation that would guarantee their continued tax revenues.

Finally, the analysis of revenue losses from import duties clearly demonstrated how e-commerce crosses existing conceptual boundaries between (i) customs duties and domestic taxation; (ii) goods and services; and (iii) international and domestic e-commerce and its taxation. Traditional classifications and concepts in international trade become blurred in the era of e-commerce; instead, new approaches to regulating tariff and tax regimes need to be developed. Attempts at harmonizing Internet taxation rules are currently under way in many forums. Developing countries are advised to follow these debates closely and adjust their own legislation to accommodate e-commerce. This could include adaptation to OECD agreements, harmonization at the international level and entering into bilateral treaties to attract e-businesses.

REFERENCES

Bleuel, J. and M. Stewen (2000). "Value Added Taxes on Electronic Commerce: Obstacles to the EU Commission's Approach", in *INTERECONOMICS*, July/August 2000, pp. 155-161.

Bureau of National Affairs, Inc. (various years). *International Trade Reporter. Shipping Manual,* Washington D.C.

Drake, W.J. and K. Nicolaidis (1999). "Global Electronic Commerce and the General Agreement on Trade in Services: The "Millennium Round" and Beyond", in P. Sauve and R.M. Stern (eds.*), GATS 2000: New Directions in Services Trade*, Washington, D.C.: Brookings Institution Press.

European Commission (2000). *Proposal for a Regulation of the European Parliament and of the Council amending Regulation (EEC) No 218/92 on administrative co-operation in the field of indirect taxation (VAT) and Proposal for a Council Directive amending Directive 77/388/EEC as regards the value added tax arrangements applicable to certain services supplied by electronic mean*, COM (2000) 349 final, 7 June 2000, Brussels.

European Commission (1999). *Indirect Taxes and E-commerce*, Working Paper, Working Party No.1, DG XXI, June 1999, Brussels.

European Commission (1998). *Financing the European Union. Commission Report on the Operation of the Own Resources System*, DGXIX, October 1998, Brussels, www.europa.eu.int/comm/dg19/agenda2000/ownresources/html/index.htm.

European Commission (1997). *VAT in the European Community*, XXI/541/97, EC, DGXXI, January 1997, Brussels.

GATT (1994). *The Results of the Uruguay Round of Multilateral Trade Negotiations. The Legal Texts*, Geneva.

GATT (1986). *General Agreement on Tariffs and Trade*, Text of the General Agreement, Geneva.

Goolsbee, A. (1999). *In a World without Borders: The Impact of Taxes on Internet Commerce*, National Bureau of Economic Research (NBER) Working Paper No. 6863, Cambridge, MA.

Heeks, R. (1998). *The Uneven Profile of Indian Software Exports*, Development Informatics Working Paper Series, No. 3, Institute of Development Policy and Management, University of Manchester, Manchester.

Hill, T.P. (1977). "On Goods and Services", in *Review of Income and Wealth*, 24(4), pp.315-338.

IFO Institute for Economic Research (1999). *Import Documentation Requirements*, various country reports, Munich.

ITU (1999). *Challenges to the Network: Internet for Development*, February 1999, Geneva.

Kerrigan, A. (1999). "Taxation of E-commerce. Recent developments from a European Perspective", in *Wirtschaftspolitische Blätter*, 5/1999, pp. 439-447.

KPMG (various years). *Country Tax Facts*, http://www.tax.kpmg.net/ country_tax facts/ default.htm.

Lukas, A. (1999). *Tax Bytes: A Primer on the Taxation of Electronic Commerce*, Cato Institute Trade Policy Analysis No.9, Washington, D.C.

OECD (2000). *The Application of the Permanent Establishment Definition in the Context of Electronic Commerce: Proposed Clarification of the Commentary on Article 5 of the OECD Model Tax Convention*, Revised Draft for Comments, OECD, March 2000, Paris.

OECD (1999a). *Business-to-business Electronic Commerce: Status, Economic Impact and Policy Implications*, DSTI/ICCP/IE(99)4/FINAL, 11 October 1999, Paris.

OECD (1999b). *Progress Report: Taxation and Electronic Commerce*, Technology Technical Advisory Group (TAG) Report, October 1999, Paris.

OECD (1998a) *Electronic Commerce: Taxation Framework Conditions*, DAFE/CFA

(98)50, Paris, www.oecd.org/daf/fa/e_com/ottawa.htm.

OECD (1998b). *Electronic Commerce: A Discussion Paper on Taxation Issues*, 17 September 1998, http://www.oecd.org/daf/fa/e_com/discusse.pdf.

Owen, J.(1997). "What Chance for the Virtual Taxman?" in *The OECD Observer*, No. 208, October/November 1997, pp.16-19.

Panagariya, A. (2000). *E-Commerce, Developing Countries and the WTO*, UNCTAD Study Series on "Policy Issues on International Trade and Commodities", No. 2, UNCTAD/ITCD/TAB/2, Geneva.

Schuknecht, L. (1999). *A Quantitative Assessment of Electronic Commerce*, WTO Working Paper ERAD-99-01, September 1999, Geneva.

The Economist (2000a), *Internet Economics*, 1 April 2000

The Economist (2000b), *A Survey of E-commerce*, 26 February 2000.

The Economist (2000c), *A Survey of Globalisation and Tax*, 29 January 2000.

Teltscher, S. (2000). *Tariffs, Taxes and Electronic Commerce: Revenue Implications for Developing Countries*, UNCTAD Study Series on "Policy Issues in International Trade and Commodities" No. 5, UNCTAD/ITCD/TAB/5, Geneva.

UNCTAD (1998). *Policy Issues Relating to Access to Participation in Electronic Commerce*, TD/B/Com.3/16, 17 September 1998, Geneva.

UNCTAD (1996). *Incentives and Foreign Direct Investment*, UNCTAD/DTCI/28, Current Studies, Series A, No. 30, Geneva.

Wall Street Journal Europe, *Easy on the E-Tax*, 7 October 1999.

WTO (various years), *Trade Policy Review*, Geneva.

WTO (1999a). *Preparations for the 1999 Ministerial Conference. WTO Work Programme on Electronic Commerce*, Communication from the European Communities and their Member States, WT/GC/W/306, 9 August 1999, Geneva.

WTO (1999b). *Work Programme on Electronic Commerce. Progress Report to the General Council*, S/L/74, 27 July 1999, Geneva.

WTO (1999c). *Work Programme on Electronic Commerce. Information provided to the General Council*, G/C/W/158, 26 July 1999, Geneva.

WTO (1999d). *Report of the Meeting held on 22 and 24 June 1999*, S/C/M/37, 20 July 1999, Geneva.

WTO (1999e). *Report of the Meeting held on 18 May 1999*, S/C/M/36, 15 June 1999, Geneva.

WTO (1999f). *Work Programme on Electronic Commerce*, Submission by the United States, WT/GC/16, 12 February 1999, Geneva.

WTO (1998). *Global Electronic Commerce*, Proposal by the United States, WT/GC/W/78, 9 February 1998, Geneva.

ANNEX 1:

FIGURES

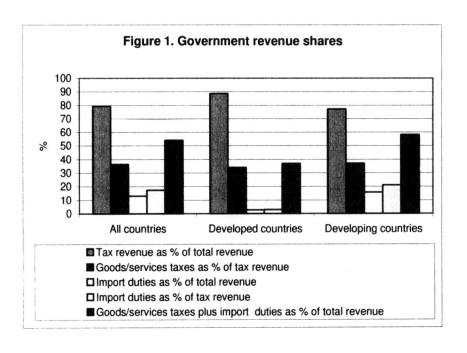

Figure 1. Government revenue shares

Legend:
- ▨ Tax revenue as % of total revenue
- ■ Goods/services taxes as % of tax revenue
- ☐ Import duties as % of total revenue
- ☐ Import duties as % of tax revenue
- ■ Goods/services taxes plus import duties as % of total revenue

32

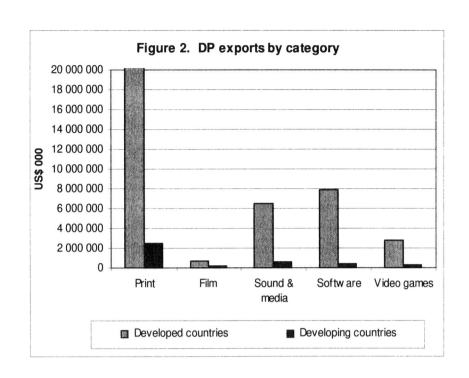

Figure 2. DP exports by category

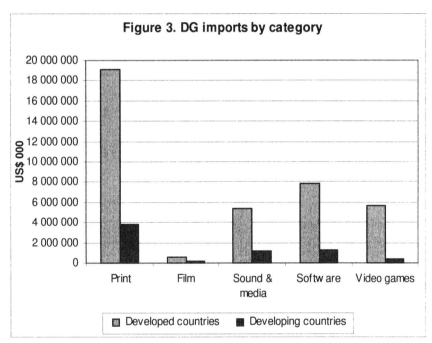

Figure 3. DG imports by category

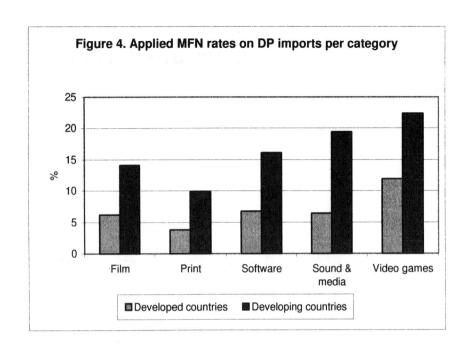

Figure 4. Applied MFN rates on DP imports per category

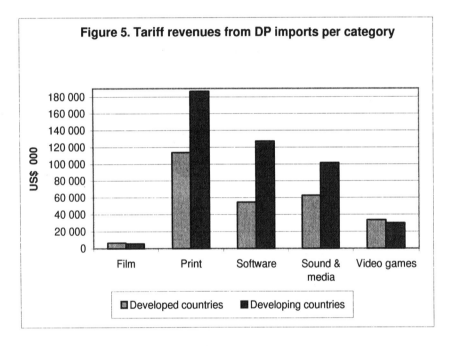

Figure 5. Tariff revenues from DP imports per category

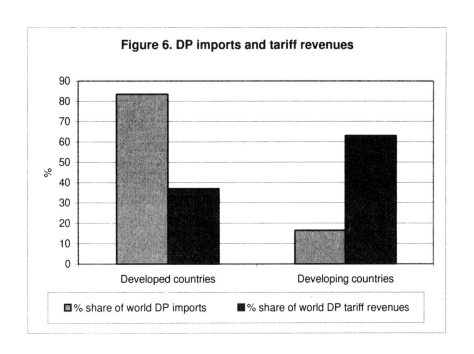

Figure 6. DP imports and tariff revenues

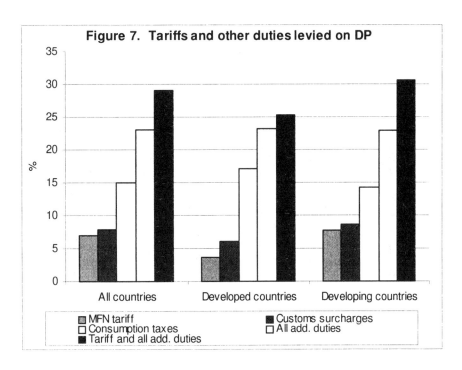

Figure 7. Tariffs and other duties levied on DP

35

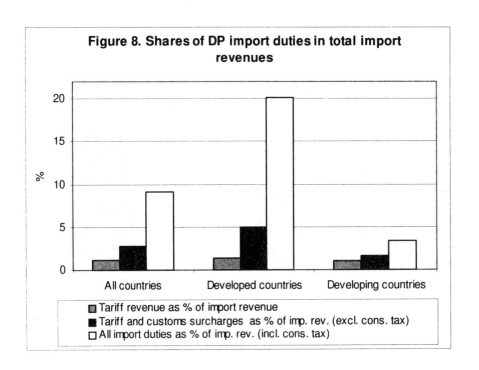

Figure 8. Shares of DP import duties in total import revenues

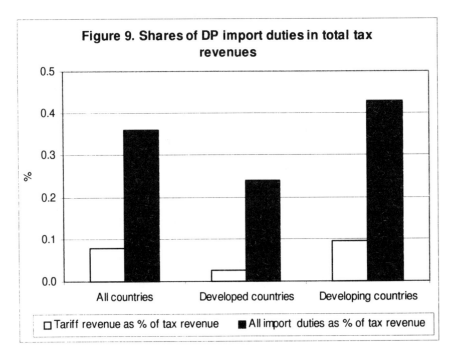

Figure 9. Shares of DP import duties in total tax revenues

ANNEX 2:

TABLES

Table 1. Government revenue shares

Country	Year	Tax revenue as % of total rev.	Goods/services taxes as % of tax rev.	Import duties as % of total rev.	Import duties as % of tax rev.	Goods/services taxes plus imp. duties as % of total rev.
Australia	1997	92.6	22.2	2.4	2.6	24.8
Bulgaria	1997	77.4	33.1	6.3	8.2	41.3
Canada	1995	88.7	20.0	1.9	2.1	22.1
Croatia	1997	94.2	41.1	8.8	9.4	50.5
Czech Republic	1997	96.2	35.6	2.7	2.8	38.4
Estonia	1997	87.6	46.9	0.0	0.0	46.9
EU15	1997	90.7	29.0	0.6	0.6	29.7
Hungary	1997	87.0	37.2	5.0	5.8	43.0
Iceland	1997	85.3	57.4	1.2	1.4	58.8
Israel	1997	86.5	37.0	0.4	0.5	37.5
Japan	1993	84.0	17.2	1.0	1.1	18.3
Latvia	1997	86.1	47.0	2.0	2.3	49.4
Lithuania	1997	95.6	51.9	2.7	2.8	54.6
New Zealand	1997	91.4	28.9	2.7	3.0	31.9
Norway	1997	78.8	45.1	0.5	0.7	45.8
Poland	1997	90.7	35.5	4.1	4.5	40.0
Romania	1997	88.9	29.2	5.6	6.3	35.5
Russian Federation	1995	87.8	38.8	2.8	3.2	42.0
Switzerland	1997	92.7	24.6	1.0	1.1	25.7
United States	1997	92.4	3.6	1.1	1.2	4.8
Total developed countries[1]		**88.7**	**34.1**	**2.6**	**3.0**	**37.0**
Albania	1997	79.5	44.8	18.0	22.6	67.4
Algeria	1996	95.3	10.9	15.5	16.3	27.2
Argentina	1997	91.2	44.6	6.6	7.2	51.9
Azerbaijan	1997	95.2	43.2	6.4	6.7	50.0
Bahamas	1997	90.3	1.6	47.4	52.5	54.1
Bahrain	1997	24.4	12.7	8.8	35.9	48.5
Belarus	1997	94.7	43.0	7.6	8.0	51.0
Belize	1997	88.7	40.3	29.5	33.2	73.5
Bhutan	1997	35.8	36.8	0.9	2.5	39.3
Bolivia	1997	88.4	58.7	6.7	7.5	66.2
Brazil	1994	64.9	32.6	1.7	2.6	35.2
Burundi	1997	92.7	48.4	14.1	15.2	63.6
Cameroon	1995	72.6	34.6	19.7	27.1	61.8
Chile	1997	83.1	55.5	8.4	10.1	65.5
China	1997	97.4	78.0	7.4	7.6	85.6
Colombia	1997	86.0	49.8	8.1	9.4	59.2
Congo, Dem. Rep. of the	1997	80.3	22.8	26.1	32.5	55.3
Congo	1997	22.5	21.0	8.8	39.1	60.0
Costa Rica	1996	87.9	45.5	6.9	7.9	53.4
Côte d'Ivoire	1997	96.2	17.4	30.7	31.9	49.3
Cyprus	1997	78.1	34.2	5.6	7.1	41.3
Dominican Republic	1997	91.1	37.5	33.1	36.3	73.8
Ecuador	1994	88.3	29.2	10.4	11.8	41.0
Egypt	1997	58.3	27.2	11.6	19.9	47.2
El Salvador	1997	91.7	57.4	11.6	12.7	70.1
Ethiopia	1995	68.3	21.3	20.0	29.2	50.5
Fiji	1996	86.1	37.6	19.6	22.8	60.4
Gambia	1993	94.0	34.5	41.9	44.5	79.0
Georgia	1997	75.5	71.4	12.6	16.6	88.0
Ghana	1993	77.4	43.8	20.2	26.1	69.8
Grenada	1995	84.0	49.5	16.8	20.0	69.5
Guatemala	1997	97.5	57.2	16.0	16.4	73.6

/...

Country	Year	Tax revenue as % of total rev.	Goods/services taxes as % of tax rev.	Import duties as % of total rev.	Import duties as % of tax rev.	Goods/services taxes plus imp. duties as % of total rev.
India	1997	74.7	35.3	21.4	28.6	63.9
Indonesia	1997	91.1	30.7	2.6	2.9	33.5
Iran, Islamic Rep. of	1997	38.1	20.0	6.2	16.3	36.3
Jordan	1997	74.6	41.6	21.3	28.6	70.1
Kazakhstan	1997	78.5	29.3	1.8	2.3	31.6
Kenya	1996	86.5	43.0	14.8	17.1	60.2
Korea, Rep. of	1997	85.3	39.1	6.3	7.4	46.5
Kuwait	1997	2.5	0.9	2.0	76.9	77.8
Kyrgyzstan	1997	79.3	68.4	5.1	6.4	74.8
Lebanon	1997	77.1	8.5	46.4	60.2	68.6
Madagascar	1996	97.7	24.9	52.0	53.2	78.1
Malaysia	1997	81.9	32.2	10.9	13.3	45.5
Maldives	1997	52.2	31.6	33.4	64.0	95.5
Malta	1997	84.7	39.8	4.1	4.8	44.6
Mauritius	1997	82.8	34.6	30.5	36.8	71.4
Mexico	1997	88.4	67.3	3.9	4.4	71.7
Mongolia	1997	75.1	35.6	4.2	5.6	41.2
Morocco	1995	81.8	46.9	14.4	17.6	64.6
Myanmar	1997	57.0	51.4	9.9	17.3	68.7
Nepal	1997	83.4	44.7	27.7	33.2	77.8
Nicaragua	1995	92.4	45.6	20.6	22.2	67.9
Oman	1997	28.6	4.5	2.3	8.2	12.7
Pakistan	1997	80.5	35.9	22.4	27.8	63.7
Panama	1997	72.3	25.1	10.2	14.1	39.2
Papua New Guinea	1994	85.8	12.2	17.5	20.3	32.5
Paraguay	1993	64.5	55.4	12.5	19.3	74.7
Peru	1997	87.1	55.8	8.4	9.7	65.4
Philippines	1997	87.7	32.4	20.2	23.0	55.4
Rwanda	1993	91.2	38.9	31.8	34.8	73.7
Saint Kitts and Nevis	1994	77.5	14.1	34.2	44.2	58.2
Saint Vincent and the Gre.	1997	85.9	11.9	40.7	47.4	59.3
Seychelles	1997	74.9	9.9	41.3	55.1	65.1
Sierra Leone	1997	96.7	34.0	45.9	47.4	81.4
Singapore	1997	42.3	29.4	0.8	2.0	31.4
South Africa	1997	94.1	37.1	0.2	0.2	37.3
Sri Lanka	1997	86.4	61.6	16.2	18.8	80.4
Syrian Arab Republic	1997	67.8	30.6	8.0	11.9	42.4
Thailand	1997	89.3	47.4	11.9	13.3	60.7
Trinidad and Tobago	1995	83.4	30.5	5.6	6.7	37.2
Tunisia	1996	83.5	24.9	24.9	29.8	54.7
Turkey	1997	86.8	49.5	2.3	2.7	52.2
United Arab Emirates	1997	21.2	91.4	0.0	0.0	91.4
Uruguay	1997	91.9	43.6	3.3	3.6	47.1
Venezuela	1997	73.1	41.3	6.8	9.3	50.6
Viet Nam	1997	84.5	38.0	21.3	25.2	63.2
Yemen	1997	33.7	20.4	8.9	26.4	46.9
Zambia	1997	94.9	52.7	12.9	13.6	66.3
Zimbabwe	1997	87.8	26.5	16.6	19.0	45.5
Total developing countries		**77.2**	**37.1**	**15.8**	**21.2**	**58.3**
Total all countries		**79.5**	**36.5**	**13.2**	**17.5**	**54.0**

Source: International Monetary Fund, Government Finance Statistics Yearbook 1999.

[1] Includes economies in transition.

Table 2. HS codes of digitizable products

HS heading	Commodity description
37	**Film (recorded)**
3705	Photographic films
3706	Cinematographic films
49	**Printed matter**
4901	Books
4902	Newspapers
4903	Children's books
4904	Music
4905	Maps, atlases
4906	Plans (architect., eng., ind., commercial)
4907	Unused stamps
4908	Transfers
4909	Postcards
4910	Calendars
4911	Commercial catalogues, pictures, designs
8524 (except 31,40,91)	**Sound & media**
852410	Records
852432	CDs
852439	CDs
852451-53	Tapes
852460	Cards
852499	Other (recorded disks)
8524	**Software**
852431	
852440	
852491	
950410	**Video games**

Table 3. World trade in DP, 1997

	Total imports 000 US$	Total exports 000 US$	DP imports % share of total imports	DP exports % share of total exports	% share of world DP imports	% share of world DP exports	% share of world imports	% share of world exports
United States	6 719 766	8 366 199	0.7	1.3	14.6	19.6	17.3	13.2
United Kingdom	3 850 637	4 962 470	1.3	1.8	8.3	11.7	5.9	5.7
Germany	3 564 916	4 578 565	0.8	0.9	7.7	10.8	8.6	10.5
Ireland	666 317	3 321 860	1.7	6.2	1.4	7.8	0.8	1.1
Japan	2 165 979	2 501 501	0.6	0.6	4.7	5.9	6.5	8.6
France	3 168 765	2 419 110	1.2	0.9	6.9	5.7	5.1	5.8
Netherlands	1 707 722	2 169 501	1.1	1.2	3.7	5.1	3.1	3.8
Italy	1 409 717	1 573 848	0.7	0.7	3.1	3.7	4.0	4.9
Canada	3 606 180	1 326 784	1.8	0.6	7.8	3.1	3.8	4.4
Austria	1 081 737	1 242 937	1.7	2.2	2.3	2.9	1.2	1.2
Belgium-Luxembourg	1 412 834	1 198 905	0.9	0.7	3.1	2.8	3.1	3.5
Spain	1 058 685	1 163 906	0.9	1.1	2.3	2.7	2.4	2.2
Singapore	628 972	967 792	0.5	0.8	1.4	2.3	2.6	2.6
Switzerland	1 850 819	644 904	2.4	0.8	4.0	1.5	1.5	1.6
Russian Federation	556 883	575 444	0.8	0.7	1.2	1.4	1.3	1.8
Hong Kong (China)	948 820	566 277	0.4	2.1	2.1	1.3	4.1	0.6
China	715 604	540 118	0.5	0.3	1.5	1.3	2.7	3.7
Denmark	605 611	482 826	1.4	1.0	1.3	1.1	0.9	1.0
Sweden	720 956	438 434	1.1	0.5	1.6	1.0	1.2	1.7
Mexico	835 149	429 222	0.7	0.4	1.8	1.0	2.2	2.3
Finland	279 758	423 891	0.9	1.0	0.6	1.0	0.6	0.8
Korea, Rep. of	719 662	269 419	0.5	0.2	1.6	0.6	2.8	2.8
India	361 308	267 453	0.9	0.8	0.8	0.6	0.8	0.7
Australia	1 211 250	235 765	2.0	0.4	2.6	0.6	1.2	1.2
Czech Rep.	303 128	206 445	1.1	0.9	0.7	0.5	0.5	0.5
Honduras	14 814	150 792	0.6	14.6	0.0	0.4	0.0	0.0
Chile	170 234	148 873	0.9	0.9	0.4	0.3	0.3	0.3
Colombia	187 730	123 171	1.2	1.1	0.4	0.3	0.3	0.2
Argentina	344 997	118 119	1.1	0.4	0.7	0.3	0.6	0.5
Poland	343 144	112 632	0.8	0.4	0.7	0.3	0.8	0.5
Slovakia	119 004	102 037	1.2	1.2	0.3	0.2	0.2	0.2
Malaysia	236 005	101 405	0.3	0.1	0.5	0.2	1.5	1.6
Norway	589 548	81 523	1.6	0.2	1.3	0.2	0.7	1.0
Greece	235 898	76 653	0.9	0.7	0.5	0.2	0.5	0.2
Slovenia	63 574	66 274	0.7	0.8	0.1	0.2	0.2	0.2
Israel	232 324	65 391	0.8	0.3	0.5	0.2	0.6	0.5
Thailand	263 800	63 768	0.4	0.1	0.6	0.1	1.2	1.2
Portugal	325 835	62 177	0.9	0.3	0.7	0.1	0.7	0.5
Hungary	111 836	50 032	0.5	0.3	0.2	0.1	0.4	0.4
Brazil	518 631	42 055	0.8	0.1	1.1	0.1	1.3	1.1
South Africa	390 505	38 198	1.3	0.2	0.8	0.1	0.6	0.5
Malta	32 126	36 823	1.3	2.5	0.1	0.1	0.0	0.0
Turkey	152 739	33 930	0.3	0.1	0.3	0.1	0.9	0.5
New Zealand	363 152	32 831	2.5	0.2	0.8	0.1	0.3	0.3
Philippines	128 518	27 269	0.3	0.1	0.3	0.1	0.7	0.5
Latvia	22 484	23 805	0.8	1.4	0.0	0.1	0.1	0.0
Lithuania	30 623	18 928	0.5	0.5	0.1	0.0	0.1	0.1

/...

41

	Total imports 000 US$	Total exports 000 US$	DP imports % share of total imports	DP exports % share of total exports	% share of world DP imports	% share of world DP exports	% share of world imports	% share of world exports
Indonesia	66 958	13 219	0.2	0.0	0.1	0.0	0.8	1.1
Costa Rica	46 885	13 043	1.0	0.3	0.1	0.0	0.1	0.1
Croatia	65 411	12 436	0.7	0.3	0.1	0.0	0.2	0.1
Uruguay	13 266	8 874	0.4	0.3	0.0	0.0	0.1	0.1
Estonia	25 422	7 926	0.6	0.3	0.1	0.0	0.1	0.1
Venezuela	147 008	7 748	1.1	0.0	0.3	0.0	0.3	0.5
Egypt	32 012	7 137	0.2	0.2	0.1	0.0	0.3	0.1
Bulgaria	10 932	6 967	0.2	0.1	0.0	0.0	0.1	0.1
Peru	91 599	6 131	1.1	0.1	0.2	0.0	0.2	0.1
Barbados	16 555	6 058	1.7	2.1	0.0	0.0	0.0	0.0
Morocco	65 626	5 220	0.8	0.1	0.1	0.0	0.2	0.1
Guatemala	31 434	5 210	0.8	0.2	0.1	0.0	0.1	0.0
Romania	57 895	4 849	0.5	0.1	0.1	0.0	0.2	0.2
Trinidad and Tobago	22 292	4 262	0.7	0.2	0.0	0.0	0.1	0.1
Mauritius	16 407	3 844	0.7	0.2	0.0	0.0	0.0	0.0
Albania	4 011	3 252	0.6	2.4	0.0	0.0	0.0	0.0
Tunisia	37 095	2 989	0.5	0.1	0.1	0.0	0.2	0.1
El Salvador	24 534	2 330	0.8	0.2	0.1	0.0	0.1	0.0
Oman	13 003	2 124	0.3	0.0	0.0	0.0	0.1	0.2
Cyprus	58 932	1 595	1.6	0.4	0.1	0.0	0.1	0.0
Ecuador	51 463	1 571	1.1	0.0	0.1	0.0	0.1	0.1
Algeria	22 267	1 454	0.3	0.0	0.0	0.0	0.2	0.3
Bolivia	21 091	1 330	1.1	0.1	0.0	0.0	0.0	0.0
Iceland	30 071	1 042	1.5	0.1	0.1	0.0	0.0	0.0
Macau	5 898	1 041	0.3	0.0	0.0	0.0	0.0	0.0
Paraguay	30 333	937	0.9	0.1	0.1	0.0	0.1	0.0
Jamaica	29 163	798	0.9	0.1	0.1	0.0	0.1	0.0
United Rep. of Tanzania	12 676	598	1.0	0.1	0.0	0.0	0.0	0.0
Armenia	3 657	563	0.5	0.3	0.0	0.0	0.0	0.0
Saint Kitts and Nevis	2 778	336	1.9	1.5	0.0	0.0	0.0	0.0
Greenland	4 487	113	1.2	0.0	0.0	0.0	0.0	0.0
Panama	38 990	107	1.3	0.0	0.1	0.0	0.1	0.0
Nicaragua	14 539	90	1.0	0.0	0.0	0.0	0.0	0.0
Bangladesh	10 427	61	0.2	0.0	0.0	0.0	0.1	0.1
Madagascar	8 336	52	1.5	0.0	0.0	0.0	0.0	0.0
Grenada	4 597	30	2.7	0.1	0.0	0.0	0.0	0.0
Saint Lucia	5 427	12	1.6	0.0	0.0	0.0	0.0	0.0
Belize	3 040	3	1.1	0.0	0.0	0.0	0.0	0.0
Saint Vincent	1 678	2	0.9	0.0	0.0	0.0	0.0	0.0
Developing countries	7 599 934	4 026 142	0.6	0.4	16.5	9.5	25.8	22.3
Developed countries[1]	38 576 957	38 559 474	1.0	1.0	83.5	90.5	74.2	77.7
WORLD	46 176 891	42 585 616	0.9	0.9	100.0	100.0	100.0	100.0

Source: COMTRADE.

[1] Includes economies in transition.

Table 4. Annual growth rates of trade in DP (%)[1]

Annual growth rates of DP exports

	1991	1992	1993	1994	1995	1996	1997	1998
World	0.0	44.4	22.5	24.5	18.1	21.2	4.2	21.4
Developing countries	4.2	53.0	39.8	15.2	18.3	11.3	3.5	26.1
Developed countries	-7.1	27.1	1.7	45.8	21.5	20.1	5.1	17.1
Total exports (world)	0.5	7.1	0.0	14.0	19.5	4.2	3.6	-1.3

Annual growth rates of DP imports

	1991	1992	1993	1994	1995	1996	1997	1998
World	12.2	39.9	12.2	20.9	24.9	15.1	8.8	7.2
Developing countries	9.4	52.7	21.5	25.1	26.4	16.0	11.1	4.9
Developed countries	16.5	13.0	-2.9	13.2	26.0	13.7	5.7	9.4
Total imports (world)	0.3	7.1	-1.4	13.6	19.5	5.9	2.4	-1.0

Source: COMTRADE; UNCTAD, *Handbook of International Trade and Development Statistics* (various years).

[1] Since the number of countries varies considerably among different years, average growth rates were calculated from individual country growth rates and not from changes in total import values.

Table 5. Trade in DP per commodity grouping, 1997[1]

Exports of DP per category, 1997

	World exports	DP exports	Print	Film	Sound & media	Software	Video games
Value (000 US$)	4 758 781 889	42 457 947	23 081 082	826 637	7 147 330	8 297 065	3 105 833
% share of world exports	-	0.9	0.5	0.0	0.2	0.2	0.1
% share of DP exports	-	-	54.4	1.9	16.8	19.5	7.3
% share developing countries	20.3	9.2	11.7	21.1	8.4	4.8	9.5
% share developed countries[2]	79.7	90.8	89.3	78.9	91.6	95.2	91.5

Imports of DP per category, 1997

	World imports	DP imports	Print	Film	Sound & media	Software	Video games
Value (000 US$)	4 120 719 713	38 660 172	20 154 454	563 972	6 033 805	8 619 144	3 288 797
% share of world imports	-	0.9	0.5	0.0	0.1	0.2	0.1
% share of DP imports	-	-	52.1	1.5	15.6	22.3	8.5
% share developing countries	23.4	15.0	16.6	21.3	18.1	14.1	6.0
% share developed countries[2]	76.6	85.0	83.4	78.7	81.9	85.9	94.0

Source: COMTRADE.

[1] Data based on 85 reporting countries, representing 85% of world trade.

[2] Includes economies in transition.

Table 6. Main exporters of DP per category, 1997

Film	000 US$	%	Software	000 US$	%	Print	000 US$	%	Sound	000 US$	%	Video games	000 US$	%	All DP	000 US$	%
Korea, Rep. of	107 586	13.0	United States	2 744 243	33.1	United States	4 287 362	18.6	United States	1 651 562	23.1	Japan	1 714 979	55.2	United States	8 366 199	19.7
United Kingdom	105 923	12.8	United Kingdom	2 133 611	25.7	Germany	3 172 126	13.7	United Kingdom	969 520	13.4	Netherlands	295 065	9.5	United Kingdom	4 962 470	11.7
United States	90 254	10.9	Ireland	652 606	7.9	United Kingdom	3 087 968	13.4	Austria	747 541	10.5	Germany	276 783	8.9	Germany	4 578 565	10.8
Italy	87 520	10.6	Netherlands	593 721	7.2	France	1 680 927	7.3	Netherlands	638 655	8.9	United States	203 411	6.5	Ireland	3 321 860	7.8
Japan	78 280	9.5	Germany	490 095	5.9	Italy	1 361 356	5.9	Germany	570 546	8.0	China	165 219	5.3	Japan	2 501 501	5.9
Germany	69 015	8.3	France	370 892	4.5	Spain	999 395	4.3	Ireland	429 578	6.0	United Kingdom	156 453	5.0	France	2 419 110	5.7
Canada	59 448	7.2	Singapore	326 073	3.9	Canada	935 709	4.1	France	288 685	4.0	Mexico	72 816	2.3	Netherlands	2 169 501	5.1
France	43 373	5.2	Canada	108 907	1.3	Belgium-Lux.	921 453	4.0	Japan	222 673	3.1	Belgium-Lux.	42 165	1.4	Italy	1 573 848	3.7
India	22 846	2.8	Sweden	103 584	1.2	Netherlands	638 848	2.8	India	207 953	2.9	Canada	39 348	1.3	Canada	1 326 784	3.1
Switzerland	22 399	2.7	Japan	102 823	1.2	Singapore	533 383	2.3	Canada	183 372	2.6	France	35 233	1.1	Austria	1 242 937	2.9
Belgium-Lux.	20 596	2.5	Denmark	98 779	1.2	Hong Kong (China)	499 897	2.2	Belgium-Lux.	121 046	1.7	Spain	33 558	1.1	Belgium-Lux.	1 198 905	2.8
China	14 019	1.7	Belgium-Lux.	93 645	1.1	Switzerland	452 792	2.0	Switzerland	104 156	1.5	Malaysia	10 309	0.3	Spain	1 163 906	2.7
Austria	13 332	1.6	Austria	82 106	1.0	Russian Fed.	443 132	1.9	Sweden	91 900	1.3	Ireland	9 154	0.3	Singapore	967 792	2.3
Singapore	10 604	1.3	Switzerland	62 377	0.8	Austria	394 346	1.7	Singapore	91 408	1.3	Italy	8 325	0.3	Switzerland	644 904	1.5
Denmark	10 055	1.2	Russian Fed.	44 339	0.5	Japan	382 746	1.7	Russian Fed.	85 428	1.2	Singapore	6 323	0.2	Russian Fed.	575 444	1.4
Spain	9 429	1.1	Spain	37 627	0.5	Finland	354 670	1.5	Spain	83 898	1.2	Sweden	5 681	0.2	Hong Kong (China)	566 277	1.3
Finland	9 331	1.1	Italy	36 299	0.4	China	310 736	1.3	Italy	80 347	1.1	Austria	5 611	0.2	China	540 118	1.3
Hong Kong (China)	5 948	0.7	Finland	33 633	0.4	Denmark	299 993	1.3	Mexico	78 749	1.1	Finland	3 535	0.1	Denmark	482 826	1.1
Israel	5 743	0.7	Greece	24 276	0.3	Mexico	267 495	1.2	Denmark	72 249	1.0	Switzerland	3 181	0.1	Sweden	438 434	1.0
Argentina	5 641	0.7	Poland	16 463	0.2	Sweden	231 826	1.0	Australia	48 244	0.7	Korea, Rep. of	2 382	0.1	Mexico	429 222	1.0
Sweden	5 444	0.7	Czech Rep.	15 562	0.2	Australia	169 692	0.7	Hong Kong (China)	46 115	0.6	Hong Kong (China)	2 343	0.1	Finland	423 891	1.0
Australia	5 104	0.6	Korea, Rep. of	14 619	0.2	Czech Rep.	158 394	0.7	China	42 611	0.6	Greece	2 313	0.1	Korea, Rep. of	269 419	0.6
Ireland	4 813	0.6	Hong Kong (China)	11 975	0.1	Honduras	150 751	0.7	Korea, Rep. of	37 715	0.5	South Africa	1 942	0.1	India	267 453	0.6
Mexico	3 354	0.4	Australia	11 208	0.1	Ireland	134 073	0.6	Czech Rep.	30 804	0.4	Denmark	1 749	0.1	Australia	235 597	0.6
Netherlands	3 212	0.4	Hungary	9 442	0.1	Chile	122 378	0.5	Norway	26 897	0.4	Indonesia	1 535	0.0	Czech Rep.	206 445	0.5
New Zealand	1 761	0.2	Norway	9 026	0.1	Korea, Rep. of	107 117	0.5	Finland	22 722	0.3	Australia	1 349	0.0	Honduras	150 792	0.4
Czech Rep.	1 519	0.2	Malaysia	8 580	0.1	Colombia	103 357	0.4	Israel	20 840	0.3	Russian Fed.	1 216	0.0	Chile	148 873	0.4
South Africa	1 380	0.2	China	7 534	0.1	Argentina	97 473	0.4	Malaysia	18 513	0.3	Norway	853	0.0	Colombia	122 854	0.3
Russian Fed.	1 329	0.2	Chile	7 270	0.1	Slovakia	94 369	0.4	Colombia	18 246	0.3	Malta	759	0.0	Argentina	118 119	0.3
World	826 637		World	8 297 065		World	23 081 082		World	7 147 330		World	3 105 833		World	42 457 947	

Source: COMTRADE.

45

Table 7. Main importers of DP per category, 1997

Film	000 US$	%	Software	000 US$	%	Print	000 US$	%	Sound	000 US$	%	Video games	000 US$	%	All DP	000 US$	%
United States	145 423	25.8	Germany	1 052 053	12.2	United Kingdom	2 832 333	14.1	United States	731 369	12.1	United States	2 735 029	83.2	United States	6 719 766	17.4
Korea, Rep. of	75 630	13.4	United Kingdom	838 180	9.7	United States	2 199 749	10.9	Netherlands	495 492	8.2	United Kingdom	608 181	18.5	United Kingdom	3 850 637	10.0
France	57 850	10.3	France	791 579	9.2	Japan	1 864 983	9.3	Germany	491 731	8.1	Canada	535 317	16.3	Canada	3 606 180	9.3
Germany	52 524	9.3	Canada	714 691	8.3	Germany	1 636 196	8.1	United Kingdom	468 652	7.8	Germany	381 693	11.6	Germany	3 564 916	9.2
Japan	47 237	8.4	Italy	558 482	6.5	Canada	1 456 371	7.2	France	432 162	7.2	France	278 052	8.5	France	3 168 765	8.2
United Kingdom	34 412	6.1	United States	511 490	5.9	France	1 132 866	5.6	Japan	405 089	6.7	Japan	253 958	7.7	Japan	2 165 979	5.6
Spain	26 430	4.7	Switzerland	457 325	5.3	Switzerland	936 701	4.6	Canada	224 609	3.7	Switzerland	237 727	7.2	Switzerland	1 850 819	4.8
Belgium-Lux.	23 553	4.2	Japan	436 352	5.1	Australia	844 405	4.2	Hong Kong (China)	201 661	3.3	Netherlands	184 080	5.6	Netherlands	1 707 722	4.4
Switzerland	23 553	4.2	Korea, Rep. of	420 977	4.9	India	717 922	3.6	Spain	197 778	3.3	Belgium-Lux.	140 440	4.3	Belgium-Lux.	1 412 834	3.7
Austria	22 868	4.1	Netherlands	328 523	3.8	Spain	659 236	3.3	Italy	197 629	3.3	Italy	135 841	4.1	Italy	1 409 717	3.6
Canada	21 851	3.9	Belgium-Lux.	284 834	3.3	Netherlands	591 754	2.9	Belgium-Lux.	195 912	3.2	Australia	84 707	2.6	Australia	1 211 231	3.1
Singapore	21 082	3.7	Ireland	276 796	3.2	Italy	561 384	2.8	Australia	191 885	3.2	Austria	83 688	2.5	Austria	1 081 737	2.8
Italy	13 038	2.3	Spain	240 031	2.8	Switzerland	538 377	2.7	Switzerland	175 334	2.9	Spain	45 190	1.4	Spain	1 058 685	2.7
Australia	12 719	2.3	Australia	230 980	2.7	Belgium-Lux.	506 444	2.5	China	173 145	2.9	Hong Kong (China)	40 555	1.2	Hong Kong (China)	948 820	2.5
Netherlands	12 004	2.1	Sweden	198 699	2.3	Russian Fed.	475 279	2.4	Brazil	162 675	2.7	Mexico	37 075	1.1	Mexico	835 149	2.2
Mexico	11 792	2.1	Mexico	189 662	2.2	Hong Kong (China)	465 044	2.3	Singapore	156 760	2.6	Sweden	29 199	0.9	Sweden	720 956	1.9
Israel	9 851	1.7	Austria	161 591	1.9	Spain	454 005	2.3	Sweden	155 593	2.6	Korea, Rep. of	28 167	0.9	Korea, Rep. of	719 662	1.9
Hong Kong (China)	7 944	1.4	Denmark	156 025	1.8	Brazil	445 723	2.2	Austria	130 053	2.2	China	23 762	0.7	China	715 604	1.9
Denmark	7 594	1.3	Hong Kong (China)	134 991	1.6	Sweden	357 211	1.8	Portugal	120 087	2.0	Ireland	20 463	0.6	Ireland	666 317	1.7
Poland	7 079	1.3	Argentina	128 173	1.5	New Zealand	341 876	1.7	Norway	112 131	1.9	Singapore	16 629	0.5	Singapore	628 972	1.6
Sweden	6 827	1.2	Singapore	124 683	1.4	Singapore	338 721	1.7	Ireland	100 606	1.7	Denmark	14 739	0.4	Denmark	605 611	1.6
Ireland	6 258	1.1	Finland	81 788	0.9	Denmark	328 565	1.6	Chile	97 158	1.6	Norway	14 630	0.4	Norway	589 548	1.5
Malaysia	5 998	1.1	Czech Rep.	78 709	0.8	Norway	280 880	1.4	Mexico	88 775	1.5	Russian Fed.	12 084	0.4	Russian Fed.	556 883	1.4
Norway	5 618	1.0	Norway	65 591	0.8	Poland	267 917	1.3	Greece	87 146	1.4	Brazil	10 056	0.3	Brazil	518 631	1.3
South Africa	5 340	0.9	Israel	60 391	0.7	Ireland	223 184	1.1	Argentina	83 234	1.4	South Africa	8 827	0.3	South Africa	390 505	1.0
China	4 886	0.9	Portugal	59 875	0.7	Israel	201 939	1.0	South Africa	71 904	1.2	New Zealand	6 407	0.2	New Zealand	363 152	0.9
Indonesia	4 522	0.8	Greece	59 309	0.7	Mexico	199 046	1.0	Turkey	59 435	1.0	India	6 201	0.2	India	361 308	0.9
Portugal	4 496	0.8	Russian Fed.	57 479	0.7	China	178 366	0.9	Denmark	57 289	0.9	Argentina	6 113	0.2	Argentina	344 997	0.9
Finland	3 169	0.6	South Africa	56 631	0.7	Korea, Rep. of	159 461	0.8	Poland	54 105	0.9	Poland	5 895	0.2	Poland	343 144	0.9
World	563 972		World	8 619 144		World	20 154 454		World	6 033 805		World	3 288 797		World	38 660 172	

Source: COMTRADE.

46

Table 8. Applied MFN rates on DP imports per country, 1997[1]

Country	Average MFN	Import-weighted MFN	Country	Average MFN	Import-weighted MFN
Bangladesh	58.4	31.5	Jamaica	13.8	4.6
India	23.1	27.3	Antigua and Barbuda	10.7	4.5
Pakistan	40.2	26.0	Rwanda	19.7	4.4
Solomon Islands	24.2	20.8	Panama	5.4	4.4
Egypt	30.4	20.7	Cameroon	15.1	4.4
Burkina Faso	30.3	19.7	Cuba	8.3	4.4
Morocco	17.6	17.8	Guatemala	7.8	4.3
Tunisia	23.7	17.0	Taiwan Province of China	3.4	4.0
Congo	16.0	15.5	Oman	5.0	4.0
Thailand	16.1	15.2	Malta	5.1	3.9
United Rep. of Tanzania	19.2	15.0	Trinidad and Tobago	13.1	3.9
Equatorial Guinea	11.8	14.7	Chad	13.6	3.8
Malawi	13.3	14.3	Korea, Rep. of	3.9	3.8
Algeria	15.6	13.5	Kazakhstan	8.2	3.6
Mauritius	26.7	12.6	Nigeria	14.4	3.4
Ghana	14.8	11.7	Ecuador	9.2	3.4
Kenya	24.4	11.2	Barbados	11.7	2.9
Dominican Republic	15.3	11.2	Sri Lanka	11.3	2.9
Indonesia	12.4	10.7	Madagascar	3.8	2.8
Peru	12.0	10.3	Uganda	13.3	2.3
Zimbabwe	22.8	10.2	Turkey	2.7	2.1
Paraguay	9.6	10.2	Sudan	1.9	2.1
Ethiopia	13.9	10.1	Nicaragua	5.8	2.1
Chile	10.6	10.1	Saint Vincent and the Grenadines	6.3	1.6
Viet Nam	15.7	10.1	Dominica	9.4	1.2
China	8.7	10.0	Montserrat	15.6	1.1
Albania	15.0	10.0	Saint Lucia	11.5	1.1
Mexico	12.0	9.7	Saint Kitts and Nevis	11.4	1.0
Philippines	11.4	8.9	Grenada	13.9	0.8
Colombia	8.5	8.8	Brunei	0.0	0.0
Belarus	12.3	8.6	Hong Kong (China)	0.0	0.0
South Africa	5.1	8.6	Kyrgyzstan	0.0	0.0
Venezuela	9.7	8.3	Singapore	0.0	0.0
Brazil	13.3	8.3	**Developing countries**	**13.1**	**7.7**
Malaysia	7.3	7.9			
Argentina	14.4	7.9	Ukraine	8.1	8.6
Papua New Guinea	13.8	7.7	Israel	6.8	7.5
Côte d'Ivoire	17.8	7.6	Moldova	16.5	7.2
Romania	12.1	7.1	Poland	9.2	7.0
Zambia	15.3	6.4	Russian Federation	12.0	6.3
Belize	11.7	6.3	Latvia	7.6	5.6
Uruguay	10.5	6.2	Iceland	3.9	4.3
Saudi Arabia	10.2	6.0	Czech Republic	3.4	3.2
Nepal	10.9	6.0	New Zealand	2.3	3.0
Guyana	13.8	5.8	European Union	2.4	2.0
Honduras	8.9	5.7	Canada	2.6	1.8
Costa Rica	8.9	5.2	Australia	1.6	1.8
Gabon	15.6	4.9	United States	0.6	0.3
Central African Rep.	14.4	4.9	Norway	0.1	0.0
Mali	15.0	4.8	Estonia	0.0	0.0
Bolivia	9.0	4.8	Japan	0.0	0.0
Suriname	11.3	4.7	Lithuania	0.0	0.0
El Salvador	8.8	4.7	Switzerland	0.0	0.0
Hungary	5.1	4.7	**Developed countries[2]**	**4.3**	**3.2**
Mozambique	22.4	4.6	**World**	**11.6**	**7.0**

Source: TRAINS, COMTRADE.

[1] Import data based on partner export data from 68 reporting countries.
Excludes intra-EU trade.
Excludes imports which are subject to specific tariffs.

[2] Includes economies in transition.

47

Table 9. Applied MFN rates and tariff revenues per commodity, 1997[1]

HS	Commodity description	Av. MFN (%)	Developed c.[2] (%)	Developing c. (%)	Tariff revenue 000 US$	Developed c. 000 US$	Developing c. 000 US$
37	Film						
370510	Photographic film	12.3	6.3	14.4	2 415	1 114	1 301
370520	"	11.0	3.9	13.4	462	220	242
370590	"	13.0	5.5	15.3	4 208	2 323	1 885
370610	Cinematographic film	12.3	7.8	13.8	4 606	2 296	2 310
370690	"	12.2	7.6	13.7	1 072	903	169
	Total film	**12.2**	**6.2**	**14.1**	**12 763**	**6 856**	**5 907**
49	**Printed matter**						
490110	Books	2.7	1.2	3.1	5 015	482	4 534
490191	"	2.4	0.2	3.0	2 405	5	2 400
490199	"	2.7	1.0	3.2	62 196	13 108	49 088
490210	Newspapers	3.0	1.7	3.4	995	69	926
490290	"	3.1	2.0	3.4	12 178	3 985	8 192
490300	Children's books	5.5	3.1	6.2	3 918	2 526	1 392
490400	Music	2.7	2.1	2.9	73	1	72
490510	Maps, atlases	3.7	2.5	3.1	518	272	245
490591	"	2.7	2.3	2.9	77	29	48
490599	"	3.2	2.9	3.4	558	132	426
490600	Plans (archit., eng.)	4.0	1.9	4.6	2 055	202	1 853
490700	Unused stamps	9.2	4.9	10.3	16 674	3 091	13 583
490810	Transfers	14.9	4.9	18.1	5 270	678	4 592
490890	"	15.9	6.3	18.7	13 957	2 735	11 222
490900	Postcards	20.7	9.8	23.5	25 531	15 690	9 842
491000	Calendars	19.9	8.3	22.9	7 665	4 397	3 269
491110	Commercial catalogues	14.0	5.0	16.2	61 992	41 800	20 192
491191	Pictures, designs	17.1	5.3	20.1	12 618	4 624	7 993
491199	"	16.6	7.3	19.3	67 003	20 132	46 871
	Total printed matter	**8.6**	**3.8**	**9.9**	**300 696**	**113 958**	**186 739**
85	**Software**						
852431	"	12.7	7.0	15.4	53 158	15 080	38 079
852440	"	13.8	6.6	16.9	13 038	2 354	10 684
852491	"	13.1	6.7	16.0	115 944	37 401	78 543
	Total software	**13.2**	**6.8**	**16.1**	**182 140**	**54 834**	**127 306**
85	**Sound & media**						
852410	Records	17.2	6.3	20.2	4 876	1 727	3 149
852432	CDs	16.0	6.6	19.1	28 080	12 510	15 571
852439	"	15.3	6.5	18.5	35 125	19 375	15 750
852451	Tapes	16.3	6.6	19.7	6 507	2 562	3 945
852452	"	16.7	6.2	20.1	5 641	1 765	3 875
852453	"	16.3	6.6	19.7	11 677	3 882	7 795
852460	Cards	16.0	6.1	19.4	2 131	716	1 414
852499	Other	15.7	6.6	18.8	70 605	20 434	50 171
	Total sound & media	**16.2**	**6.4**	**19.4**	**164 641**	**62 971**	**101 670**
95	**Video games**						
950410	"	20.0	11.9	22.4	64 061	33 888	30 173
	Total video games	**20.0**	**11.9**	**22.4**	**64 061**	**33 888**	**30 173**
	TOTAL				**724 302**	**272 507**	**451 795**

Source: TRAINS, COMTRADE.

[1] Import data based on partner export data from 68 reporting countries (representing 85% of world imports).
Excludes intra-EU trade.
Excludes imports which are subject to specific tariffs.
Tariff revenues calculated based on import-weighted tariffs.

[2] Includes economies in transition.

Table 10. Applied MFN rates per product grouping, top 25 countries

Country (Film)	Film Av. MFN	Film W. MFN	Country (Print)	Print Av. MFN	Print W. MFN	Country (Sound)	Sound Av. MFN	Sound W. MFN	Country (Software)	Software Av. MFN	Software W. MFN	Country (Video games)	Video games Av. MFN	Video games W. MFN
Pakistan	51.7	44.0	Bangladesh	38.4	29.8	Bangladesh	100.0	100.0	Bangladesh	100.0	100.0	Papua New Guinea	55.0	55.0
Solomon Islands	35.0	35.0	Egypt	18.7	21.4	Egypt	52.5	50.7	Egypt	50.0	42.6	Solomon Islands	50.0	50.0
Egypt	32.0	32.9	India	30.1	21.0	India	40.0	40.0	India	40.0	40.0	Kenya	50.0	50.0
Zimbabwe	34.0	31.9	Pakistan	26.3	20.5	Côte d'Ivoire	40.0	40.0	Côte d'Ivoire	30.0	30.0	Algeria	45.0	45.0
Burkina Faso	31.0	31.0	Zimbabwe	22.4	19.1	United Rep. of Tanzania	37.5	35.5	United Rep. of Tanzania	30.0	30.0	Malawi	40.0	40.0
Albania	30.0	30.0	Mozambique	14.8	17.4	Zambia	35.0	35.0	Zambia	25.0	25.0	Nepal	40.0	40.0
Chad	30.0	30.0	Tunisia	9.0	17.2	Argentina	33.7	34.1	Argentina	23.0	24.7	Zimbabwe	40.0	40.0
Mali	30.0	30.0	Kenya	12.6	16.8	Albania	33.0	33.8	Albania	20.0	20.0	Sri Lanka	40.0	40.0
Morocco	31.8	29.1	Côte d'Ivoire	17.0	15.6	Belarus	30.0	30.0	Belarus	20.0	20.0	China	35.0	35.0
India	25.0	25.0	Mauritius	10.0	15.5	El Salvador	34.2	28.5	El Salvador	20.0	20.0	Mozambique	35.0	35.0
Zambia	25.0	25.0	United Rep. of Tanzania	15.5	15.3	Russian Fed.	22.8	28.4	Russian Fed.	20.0	20.0	Pakistan	35.0	35.0
Russian Fed.	25.0	25.0	Jamaica	10.6	15.2	Zimbabwe	26.4	26.6	Zimbabwe	20.0	20.0	Tunisia	35.0	35.0
Cameroon	18.0	23.4	Dominican Rep.	14.1	14.0	Brazil	23.1	26.5	Brazil	19.0	19.0	Burkina Faso	33.0	33.0
Romania	22.0	22.7	Ghana	16.0	13.6	Morocco	25.0	25.0	Morocco	18.8	18.8	Albania	31.0	31.0
Mozambique	24.0	22.6	Zambia	12.0	12.0	Uruguay	25.0	25.0	Uruguay	16.0	16.0	Belarus	30.0	30.0
Ghana	28.1	20.4	Argentina	7.9	11.8	South Africa	21.3	23.5	South Africa	11.0	15.1	Cameroon	30.0	30.0
Nepal	20.0	20.0	Trinidad and Tobago	20.1	11.2	Algeria	22.8	22.7	Algeria	15.0	15.0	Central African Rep.	30.0	30.0
Cote d'Ivoire	20.0	20.0	Romania	14.7	10.8	Congo	22.6	20.4	Congo	15.0	15.0	Chad	30.0	30.0
Indonesia	21.7	19.3	Albania	10.4	10.6	Venezuela	20.0	20.0	Venezuela	13.3	14.8	Congo	30.0	30.0
Gabon	19.0	19.2	Belarus	14.3	10.4	Nepal	20.0	20.0	Nepal	17.5	14.0	Dominican Rep.	30.0	30.0
Kenya	25.0	18.5	Indonesia	12.7	10.0	Poland	20.0	20.0	Poland	14.1	14.0	Gabon	30.0	30.0
Equatorial Guinea	24.3	18.2	Russia	10.2	9.5	Mexico	20.0	20.0	Mexico	14.2	13.7	Côte d'Ivoire	30.0	30.0
Ethiopia	12.5	17.5	Philippines	11.7	8.9	Malaysia	17.7	19.7	Malaysia	10.0	13.7	Kazakhstan	30.0	30.0
United Rep. of Tanzania	21.7	17.5	Nepal	19.4	8.9	Indonesia	16.3	19.3	Indonesia	15.0	13.3	Latvia	30.0	30.0
Thailand	15.4	17.3	Brazil	6.7	8.8	China	19.0	19.0	China	9.9	12.4	Mali	30.0	30.0

Source: TRAINS, COMTRADE.

49

Table 11. Tariff revenue losses from DP imports per country

Country	DP tariff revenue weighted, 000 US$	DP tariff revenue as % of total rev.	DP tariff rev. as % of imp.rev.	DP tariff rev. as % of tax rev.
Albania	434	0.12	0.66	0.15
Algeria	2 370	0.02	0.10	0.02
Argentina	23 054	0.06	0.88	0.06
Australia	16 123	0.02	0.66	0.02
Belarus	596	0.01	0.17	0.01
Belize	103	0.07	0.25	0.08
Bolivia	897	0.07	1.00	0.08
Brazil	46 518	0.03	1.62	0.04
Cameroon	503	0.05	0.24	0.06
Canada	61 764	0.05	2.85	0.06
Chile	10 393	0.06	0.71	0.07
China	40 747	0.08	1.06	0.08
Colombia	12 745	0.10	1.17	0.11
Congo	490	0.07	0.81	0.32
Costa Rica	1 282	0.05	0.77	0.06
Côte d'Ivoire	1 947	0.08	0.28	0.09
Czech Republic	11 323	0.06	2.41	0.07
Dominican Republic	2 477	0.10	0.29	0.10
Ecuador	2 337	0.09	0.86	0.10
Egypt	11 160	0.05	0.45	0.09
El Salvador	722	0.06	0.48	0.06
Estonia	0	0.00	0.00	0.00
Ethiopia	1 440	0.14	0.70	0.20
European Union 15	81 577	0.00	0.48	0.00
Ghana	2 699	0.27	1.32	0.34
Grenada	12	0.02	0.10	0.02
Guatemala	926	0.06	0.36	0.06
Hungary	6 151	0.04	0.71	0.04
Iceland	1 021	0.05	3.95	0.05
India	73 870	0.14	0.66	0.19
Indonesia	5 466	0.01	0.53	0.02
Israel	11 539	0.03	6.39	0.03
Japan	0	0.00	0.00	0.00
Kazakhstan	472	0.01	0.66	0.02
Kenya	1 815	0.07	0.49	0.08
Korea, Rep. of	16 236	0.02	0.27	0.02
Kyrgyzstan	0	0.00	0.00	0.00
Latvia	1 087	0.06	2.86	0.07
Lithuania	0	0.00	0.00	0.00
Madagascar	172	0.05	0.10	0.05
Malaysia	20 072	0.09	0.80	0.11
Malta	985	0.09	2.12	0.10
Mauritius	2 052	0.24	0.77	0.28
Mexico	49 463	0.08	2.16	0.09
Morocco	9 952	0.10	0.71	0.12
Nepal	160	0.03	0.11	0.04
New Zealand	7 232	0.01	0.53	0.02
Nicaragua	149	0.03	0.15	0.03
Norway	64	0.00	0.02	0.00

/...

Country	DP tariff revenue weighted, 000 US$	DP tariff revenue as % of total rev.	DP tariff rev. as % of imp.rev.	DP tariff rev. as % of tax rev.
Oman	326	0.01	0.29	0.02
Pakistan	5 053	0.05	0.24	0.07
Panama	936	0.04	0.42	0.06
Papua New Guinea	636	0.05	0.30	0.06
Paraguay	6 113	0.65	5.21	1.01
Peru	6 333	0.06	0.72	0.07
Philippines	8 556	0.05	0.27	0.06
Poland	24 527	0.05	1.14	0.05
Romania	3 445	0.04	0.65	0.04
Russian Federation	33 954	0.05	1.71	0.05
Rwanda	127	0.06	0.20	0.07
Singapore	0	0.00	0.00	0.00
South Africa	23 257	0.06	4.11	0.07
Sri Lanka	564	0.02	0.12	0.02
Saint Kitts and Nevis	25	0.04	0.11	0.05
Saint Vincent and the Grenadines	14	0.02	0.04	0.02
Switzerland	0	0.00	0.00	0.00
Thailand	20 079	0.07	0.60	0.08
Trinidad and Tobago	448	0.03	0.52	0.03
Tunisia	5 373	0.09	0.37	0.11
Turkey	2 420	0.01	0.25	0.01
United States	10 354	0.00	0.06	0.00
Uruguay	2 712	0.04	1.29	0.05
Venezuela	11 560	0.06	0.81	0.08
Viet Nam	1 437	0.03	0.12	0.03
Zambia	581	0.08	0.62	0.08
Zimbabwe	1 878	0.07	0.44	0.08
Total	**712 868**	**0.06**	**0.86**	**0.08**
Total developed countries	**264 008**	**0.02**	**1.39**	**0.03**
Total developing countries	**449 293**	**0.07**	**0.70**	**0.09**

Source: UNCTAD calculations.

Table 12. Imports of DP covered by the ITA, ITA signatory countries

	Tariff revenue DP covered by ITA US$ 000	Tariff revenue all DP US$ 000
Australia	2 083	16 123
Canada	26 985	61 764
Czech Republic	677	11 323
El Salvador	46	722
European Union	65 359	81 577
Hong Kong (China)	0	0
Iceland	537	1 021
India	46 635	73 870
Indonesia	2 648	5 466
Israel	4 617	11 539
Japan	0	0
Korea, Rep. of	10 814	16 236
Latvia	16	1 087
Lithuania	0	0
Malaysia	14 221	20 072
New Zealand	0	7 232
Norway	0	64
Panama	671	5 053
Philippines	1 564	8 556
Poland	13 584	24 527
Romania	1 226	3 445
Singapore	0	0
Taiwan Province of China	4 923	16 858
Thailand	3 117	20 079
Turkey	971	2 420
United States	2 666	10 354
ITA all countries	**203 361**	**399 385**
ITA developing countries	**86 837**	**172 776**
All countries		**751 005**
All developing countries		**482 233**

Source: WTO, TRAINS, COMTRADE.

Table 13. Tariffs, additional duties and taxes levied on DP imports, by country

Country	% tariff	% customs surcharges	% consumption taxes	% all taxes	% tariff and all taxes
Albania	10.0	0.0	12.5	12.5	22.5
Algeria	13.5	80.7	21.0	101.7	115.2
Antigua and Barbuda	4.5	2.5	12.0	14.5	19.0
Argentina	7.9	4.8	21.0	25.8	33.7
Australia	1.8	0.0	34.3	34.3	36.0
Bangladesh	31.5	8.0	15.0	23.0	54.5
Barbados	2.9	0.0	15.0	15.0	17.9
Belarus	8.6	1.3	15.0	16.3	24.9
Belize	6.3	0.0	15.0	15.0	21.3
Bolivia	4.8	16.5	14.9	31.5	36.3
Brazil	8.3	9.9	8.1	18.0	26.3
Brunei	0.0	0.0	0.0	0.0	0.0
Burkina Faso	19.7	10.0	15.0	25.0	44.7
Cameroon	4.4	0.0	18.7	18.7	23.1
Canada	1.8	10.3	15.0	25.3	27.1
Central African Rep.	4.9	10.0	0.0	10.0	14.9
Chad	3.8	10.2	0.0	10.2	14.0
Chile	10.1	0.0	11.3	11.3	21.5
China	10.0	0.8	15.0	15.8	25.9
Colombia	8.8	0.0	14.7	14.7	23.5
Congo	15.5	40.1	0.0	40.1	55.6
Costa Rica	5.2	1.1	13.7	14.8	20.0
Côte d'Ivoire	7.6	2.5	20.0	22.5	30.1
Cuba	4.4	0.0	0.0	0.0	4.4
Czech Republic	3.2	0.0	19.3	19.3	22.5
Dominica	1.2	6.0	14.0	20.0	21.2
Dominican Republic	11.2	13.9	42.0	55.9	67.1
Ecuador	3.4	0.9	5.1	6.0	9.4
Egypt	20.7	3.0	15.0	18.0	38.7
El Salvador	4.7	0.0	5.7	5.7	10.3
Equatorial Guinea	14.7	8.1	0.0	8.1	22.8
Estonia	0.0	0.0	17.0	17.0	17.0
Ethiopia	10.1	114.5	7.3	121.8	131.9
Belgium (Belg./Lux.)	2.0	1.1	13.3	14.4	14.6
Denmark	2.0	0.0	22.8	22.8	23.0
Germany	2.0	0.0	13.9	13.9	14.3
Greece	2.0	0.0	12.5	12.5	12.8
Spain	2.0	0.0	11.6	11.6	11.8
France	2.0	0.0	15.4	15.4	15.7
Ireland	2.0	4.2	12.5	16.7	17.0
Italy	2.0	0.0	15.8	15.8	16.1
Netherlands	2.0	0.0	15.0	15.0	15.7
Austria	2.0	0.0	14.9	14.9	15.1
Portugal	2.0	0.0	12.5	12.5	12.7
Finland	2.0	0.0	17.9	17.9	18.1
Sweden	2.0	0.0	23.0	23.0	23.3
United Kingdom	2.0	0.0	12.4	12.4	13.1
Gabon	4.9	0.0	5.3	5.3	10.3
Ghana	11.7	0.0	16.8	16.8	28.4
Grenada	0.8	5.0	20.0	25.0	25.8
Guatemala	4.3	0.0	10.4	10.4	14.8
Guyana	5.8	0.0	0.0	0.0	5.8
Honduras	5.7	0.5	7.0	7.5	13.2
Hong Kong (China)	0.0	0.0	0.0	0.0	0.0
Hungary	4.7	1.3	26.2	27.4	32.1
Iceland	4.3	0.0	24.5	24.5	28.8
India	27.3	26.0	0.0	26.0	53.3
Indonesia	10.7	0.0	11.1	11.1	21.8
Israel	7.5	66.6	29.6	96.1	103.6
Jamaica	4.6	0.0	15.0	15.0	19.6
Japan	0.0	0.0	5.0	5.0	5.0
Kazakhstan	3.6	50.2	30.8	81.0	84.5

/...

53

Country	% tariff	% customs surcharges	% consumption taxes	% all taxes	% tariff and all taxes
Kenya	11.2	0.0	16.0	16.0	27.2
Korea, Rep. of	3.8	0.0	9.5	9.5	13.3
Kyrgyzstan	0.0	75.0	35.0	110.0	110.0
Latvia	5.6	65.0	18.0	83.0	88.6
Lithuania	0.0	0.0	18.0	18.0	18.0
Madagascar	2.8	30.0	70.0	100.0	102.8
Malawi	14.3	11.4	0.0	11.4	25.8
Malaysia	7.9	0.0	10.0	10.0	17.9
Mali	4.8	0.0	0.0	0.0	4.8
Malta	3.9	0.0	0.0	0.0	3.9
Mauritius	12.6	0.0	9.0	9.0	21.6
Mexico	9.7	0.9	16.5	17.4	27.0
Montserrat	1.1	12.8	17.2	30.0	31.1
Morocco	17.8	15.3	20.0	35.3	53.0
Mozambique	4.6	7.5	36.8	44.3	48.9
Nepal	6.0	0.0	15.0	15.0	21.0
New Zealand	3.0	12.9	0.0	12.9	15.9
Nicaragua	2.1	0.0	30.0	30.0	32.1
Nigeria	3.4	8.0	2.3	10.3	13.7
Norway	0.0	0.0	23.0	23.0	23.0
Oman	4.0	0.0	0.0	0.0	4.0
Pakistan	26.0	0.0	12.5	12.5	38.5
Panama	4.4	5.9	5.2	11.1	15.5
Papua New Guinea	7.7	43.6	0.0	43.6	51.3
Paraguay	10.2	0.0	21.0	21.0	31.2
Peru	10.3	0.0	55.3	55.3	65.6
Philippines	8.9	0.0	6.4	6.4	15.3
Poland	7.0	16.1	20.7	36.8	43.8
Rep. of Moldova	7.2	0.3	21.4	21.7	28.9
Romania	7.1	5.5	23.6	29.1	36.2
Russian Federation	6.3	16.8	24.9	41.7	48.0
Rwanda	4.4	5.9	15.0	20.9	25.3
Saudi Arabia	6.0	3.5	0.0	3.5	9.5
Singapore	0.0	0.0	3.0	3.0	3.0
Slovenia	0.0	2.4	19.0	21.4	21.4
Solomon Islands	20.8	0.0	20.0	20.0	40.8
South Africa	8.1	0.0	16.0	16.0	24.1
Sri Lanka	2.9	44.6	0.0	44.6	47.5
Saint Kitts and Nevis	1.0	3.0	15.0	18.0	19.0
Saint Lucia	1.1	5.5	37.4	42.9	44.0
Saint Vincent	1.6	2.5	0.0	2.5	4.1
Sudan	2.1	0.0	0.0	0.0	2.1
Suriname	4.7	2.0	0.0	2.0	6.7
Switzerland/Lichtenstein	0.0	0.0	7.5	7.5	7.5
Taiwan Province of China	4.0	6.8	32.9	39.7	43.8
Thailand	15.2	0.0	6.7	6.7	22.0
Trinidad and Tobago	3.9	0.0	15.6	15.6	19.5
Tunisia	17.0	0.0	72.0	72.0	89.0
Turkey	2.1	0.0	23.5	23.5	25.6
Uganda	2.3	0.0	17.0	17.0	19.3
Ukraine	8.6	0.0	21.7	21.7	30.3
United Rep. of Tanzania	15.0	0.0	28.8	28.8	43.8
United States	0.3	0.0	0.0	0.0	0.3
Uruguay	6.2	9.5	23.0	32.5	38.7
Venezuela	8.3	1.0	16.5	17.5	25.8
Viet Nam	10.1	0.0	10.0	10.0	20.1
Zambia	6.4	0.0	17.5	17.5	23.9
Zimbabwe	10.2	30.0	0.0	30.0	40.2
TOTAL	**6.9**	**7.9**	**15.0**	**23.0**	**29.2**
Developed countries	**3.6**	**6.1**	**17.1**	**23.1**	**25.3**
Developing countries	**7.7**	**8.7**	**14.3**	**22.9**	**30.6**

Source: UNCTAD calculations.

Notes:

1997 Imports based on partner data, for digitizable products.

Tariffs based on applied MFN import-weighted rates.

Consumption taxes are averaged for all DP (includes exemptions and reduced rates).

All taxes refer to additional duties and taxes (incl. VAT) levied on imports; includes exemptions (e.g. books, newspapers).

Specific rates not calculated (e.g. Switzerland, Norway).

Table 14. DP revenues from tariffs, additional customs duties and taxes

Country	DP tariff revenue in US$ 000	DP cons. tax revenue in US$ 000	DP tariff and cust. surch. rev. in US$ 000	DP all tax and tariff revenue in US$ 000	DP tariff and cust. surcharges as % imp. rev.	DP all import duties, as % of imp. rev.	DP all import duties, as % of tax rev.	DP all import duties, as % of total rev.
Albania	434	541	434	975	0.6	1.4	0.2	0.2
Algeria	2 370	3 679	16 511	20 191	0.7	0.9	0.1	0.1
Antigua and Barbuda	85	229	133	361	-	-	-	-
Argentina	23 054	61 641	37 253	98 895	1.9	5.1	0.3	0.3
Australia	16 123	310 290	16 123	326 413	0.7	13.3	0.4	0.3
Austria	1 755	145 016	1 755	146 770	0.3	26.6	0.2	0.2
Bangladesh	3 231	1 539	4 052	5 592	-	-	-	-
Barbados	145	743	145	888	-	-	-	-
Belarus	596	1 039	686	1 725	0.2	0.5	0.0	0.0
Belgium (Belg./Lux.)	2 456	179 426	17 517	196 943	1.5	16.6	1.3	1.1
Belize	104	248	104	353	0.3	0.8	0.3	0.2
Bolivia	897	2 764	3 954	6 718	4.4	7.5	0.5	0.4
Brazil	46 518	45 689	102 109	147 798	3.6	5.2	0.1	0.1
Brunei	0	0	0	0	-	-	-	-
Burkina Faso	480	366	723	1 089	-	-	-	-
Cameroon	503	2 127	503	2 630	0.2	1.2	0.3	0.2
Canada	61 764	504 677	408 517	913 193	15.6	34.9	0.9	0.8
Central African Rep.	33	0	101	101	-	-	-	-
Chad	52	0	192	192	-	-	-	-
Chile	11 657	20 364	1 686	22 050	0.1	1.5	0.2	0.1
China	40 747	60 877	44 118	104 995	1.2	2.9	0.3	0.2
Colombia	12 745	21 292	12 745	34 037	1.3	3.5	0.4	0.3
Congo	490	0	1 753	1 753	-	-	-	-
Costa Rica	1 282	3 357	1 559	4 916	0.9	2.9	0.2	0.2
Côte d'Ivoire	1 947	5 116	2 587	7 703	-	-	-	-
Cuba	455	0	455	455	-	-	-	-
Czech Republic	11 323	68 100	11 323	79 423	2.4	16.9	0.5	0.4
Denmark	1 249	112 088	1 249	113 337	0.3	28.0	0.7	0.6
Dominica	13	146	75	221	-	-	-	-
Dominican Republic	2 477	9 292	5 547	14 839	0.8	2.2	0.8	0.7
Ecuador	2 337	3 559	2 987	6 547	1.1	2.4	0.3	0.3
Egypt	11 160	8 099	12 780	20 879	0.6	1.0	0.2	0.1
El Salvador	774	940	774	1 715	0.5	1.2	0.1	0.1
Equatorial Guinea	27	0	41	41	-	-	-	-
Estonia	0	4 747	0	4 747	0.0	-	0.3	0.3
Ethiopia	1 440	1 038	17 687	18 724	9.2	9.8	2.9	1.8
Finland	695	49 706	695	50 401	0.4	30.7	0.1	0.1
France	7 701	481 326	7 701	489 027	0.4	27.9	0.1	0.1
Gabon	515	556	515	1 071	-	-	-	-
Germany	15 850	532 892	15 850	548 742	0.4	14.1	0.1	0.1
Ghana	2 699	3 867	2 699	6 566	1.3	3.2	0.8	0.6
Greece	594	26 435	594	27 029	0.3	13.3	0.0	0.0
Grenada	13	317	92	409	0.7	3.2	0.6	0.5
Guatemala	926	2 224	926	3 150	0.4	1.2	0.2	0.2
Guyana	114	0	114	114	-	-	-	-
Honduras	637	778	693	1 471	-	-	-	-
Hong Kong (China)	0	0	271	271	-	-	-	-
Hungary	6 151	34 591	7 803	42 395	0.9	4.9	0.3	0.2
Iceland	1 021	5 854	1 021	6 875	3.7	25.2	0.4	0.3
India	73 870	0	144 184	144 184	1.0	1.0	0.3	0.3
Indonesia	5 466	5 642	5 466	11 109	0.5	0.9	0.0	0.0
Ireland	1 712	70 457	25 493	95 950	9.9	37.1	0.5	0.4
Israel	11 539	45 802	114 585	160 387	63.5	88.9	0.4	0.4
Italy	3 338	181 985	3 338	185 324	0.3	14.4	0.0	0.0
Jamaica	692	2 274	692	2 965	-	-	-	-
Japan	0	90 188	0	90 188	0.0	1.0	0.0	0.0
Kazakhstan	472	4 079	7 130	11 208	10.0	15.8	0.4	0.3
Kenya	1 815	2 593	1 815	4 408	0.5	1.2	0.2	0.2
Korea, Rep. of	16 362	41 299	18 324	59 624	0.3	1.0	0.1	0.1
Kyrgyzstan	0	673	1 442	2 114	10.2	15.0	1.0	0.8
Latvia	1 087	3 512	13 768	17 280	36.4	45.6	1.1	0.9

/...

55

Country	DP tariff revenue in US$ 000	DP cons. tax revenue in US$ 000	DP tariff and cust. surch. rev. in US$ 000	DP all tax and tariff revenue in US$ 000	DP tariff and cust. surcharges as % imp. rev.	DP all import duties, as % of imp. rev.	DP all import duties, as % of tax rev.	DP all import duties, as % of total rev.
Lithuania	0	6 222	0	0	0.0	0.0	0.0	0.0
Luxembourg	0	-	-	0	-	0.0	0.0	0.0
Madagascar	172	4 252	1 995	6 246	1.1	3.5	1.8	1.2
Malawi	1 280	0	2 302	2 302	-	-	-	-
Malaysia	20 072	25 519	20 072	45 591	0.8	1.8	0.2	0.2
Mali	160	0	160	160	-	-	-	-
Malta	986	0	986	986	2.1	2.1	0.1	0.1
Mauritius	2 052	1 464	2 052	3 516	0.8	1.3	0.5	0.4
Mexico	49 463	84 110	54 167	138 277	2.8	7.1	0.3	0.3
Montserrat	4	66	54	120	-	-	-	-
Morocco	9 952	11 183	18 479	29 662	1.3	2.1	0.4	0.3
Mozambique	263	2 125	696	2 821	-	-	-	-
Nepal	162	407	162	569	0.1	0.3	0.1	0.1
Netherlands	17 173	354 595	17 173	371 768	0.9	19.0	0.2	0.2
New Zealand	7 232	0	37 782	37 782	2.8	2.8	0.1	0.1
Nicaragua	149	2 184	149	2 333	0.1	2.3	0.5	0.4
Nigeria	464	314	1 565	1 879	-	-	-	-
Norway	64	103 966	0	103 966	0.0	27.3	0.2	0.2
Oman	326	0	326	326	0.3	0.3	0.0	0.0
Pakistan	5 559	2 669	5 559	8 228	0.2	0.3	0.1	0.1
Panama	1 800	2 122	4 179	6 301	2.0	3.0	0.5	0.3
Papua New Guinea	636	0	4 223	4 223	2.0	2.0	0.4	0.3
Paraguay	6 113	12 632	6 113	18 746	5.1	15.5	3.0	1.9
Peru	6 333	33 828	6 333	40 161	0.7	4.6	0.4	0.4
Philippines	8 556	6 131	8 556	14 687	0.3	0.5	0.1	0.1
Poland	24 527	72 412	12 196	84 608	0.6	3.9	0.2	0.2
Portugal	906	45 526	906	46 432	-	26.3	0.1	0.1
Rep. of Moldova	407	1 219	424	1 643	-	-	-	-
Romania	3 436	11 404	6 094	17 498	1.0	3.0	0.2	0.2
Russian Federation	33 954	133 760	124 203	257 963	6.3	13.0	0.4	0.4
Rwanda	156	526	363	888	0.7	1.7	0.5	0.3
Saudi Arabia	6 559	0	10 393	10 393	-	-	-	-
Singapore	0	13 426	0	13 426	0.0	4.4	0.1	0.0
Slovenia	0	9 076	1 137	10 213	-	-	-	-
Solomon Islands	158	152	158	310	-	-	-	-
South Africa	21 914	43 179	21 914	65 093	3.9	11.5	0.2	0.2
Spain	1 788	100 910	1 788	102 698	0.2	13.2	0.1	0.1
Sri Lanka	564	0	9 284	9 284	-	-	-	-
Saint Kitts and Nevis	25	386	102	489	0.4	2.1	0.9	0.7
Saint Lucia	21	723	127	850	-	-	-	-
Saint Vincent	16	0	39	39	0.1	0.1	0.1	0.0
Sudan	59	0	59	59	-	-	-	-
Suriname	96	0	136	136	-	-	-	-
Sweden	2 445	203 284	2 445	205 729	0.3	23.3	0.2	0.2
Switzerland/Lichtenstein	0	117 164	0	117 164	0.0	19.9	0.2	0.2
Taiwan Province of China	17 064	139 683	45 930	185 612	-	-	-	-
Thailand	20 270	8 938	20 270	29 207	0.6	0.9	0.1	0.1
Trinidad and Tobago	449	1 789	449	2 238	0.5	2.7	0.2	0.1
Tunisia	5 373	22 740	5 373	28 112	0.4	1.9	0.6	0.5
Turkey	2 420	27 089	2 420	29 509	0.3	3.8	0.1	0.1
Uganda	177	1 324	177	1 501	-	-	-	-
Ukraine	4 356	11 058	4 356	15 414	-	-	-	-
United Kingdom	24 442	453 514	24 442	477 956	0.7	13.9	0.1	0.1
United Rep. of Tanzania	1 248	2 386	1 248	3 634	-	-	-	-
United States	13 594	0	13 594	13 594	0.1	0.1	0.0	0.0
Uruguay	2 712	10 141	6 901	17 043	3.3	8.1	0.3	0.3
Venezuela	11 560	22 936	12 950	35 886	0.9	2.5	0.2	0.2
Viet Nam	1 437	1 426	1 437	2 863	0.1	0.2	0.1	0.1
Zambia	581	1 594	581	2 175	0.8	3.1	0.4	0.3
Zimbabwe	2 023	0	7 950	7 950	2.9	2.9	0.6	0.5
TOTAL	**757 696**	**5 160 469**	**1 636 314**	**6 907 724**	**2.8**	**9.2**	**0.4**	**0.3**
Developed countries	**273 916**	**4 332 687**	**887 953**	**5 331 582**	**5.0**	**20.2**	**0.2**	**0.5**
Developing countries	**442 474**	**647 910**	**659 368**	**1 307 278**	**1.6**	**3.4**	**0.4**	**0.3**

Source: UNCTAD calculations.

56

UNCTAD Study Series on

POLICY ISSUES IN INTERNATIONAL TRADE AND COMMODITIES

No. 1   Erich Supper, **Is there effectively a level playing field for developing country exports?**, forthcoming.

No. 2   Arvind Pangariya, **E-commerce, WTO and developing countries**, 2000.

No. 3   Joseph Francois, **Assessing the results of general equilibrium studies of multilateral trade negotiations,** 2000.

No. 4   John Whalley, **What can the developing countries infer from the Uruguay Round models for future negotiations?**, 2000.

No. 5   Susanne Teltscher, **Tariffs, taxes and electronic commerce: Revenue implications for developing countries,** 2000.

No. 6   Bijit Bora, Peter J. Lloyd, Mari Pangestu, **Industrial policy and the WTO,** forthcoming.